Collectible Glassware from the 40's, 50's, 60's...

An Illustrated Value Guide

By Gene Florence

COLLECTOR BOOKS
A Division of Schroeder Publishing Co., Inc.

ABOUT THE AUTHOR

Gene Florence, born in Lexington in 1944, graduated from the University of Kentucky where he held a double major in mathematics and English. He taught nine years in Kentucky at the junior high and high school levels before his glass collecting "hobby" became his full-time job.

Mr. Florence has been interested in "collecting" since childhood, beginning with baseball cards and progressing through comic books, coins, bottles and finally, glassware. He first became interested in Depression glassware after purchasing an entire set of Sharon dinnerware at a garage sale for $5.00.

He has written several books on glassware: The Collector's Encyclopedia of Depression Glass in its tenth edition; *Kitchen Glassware of the Depression Years*, in its fourth edition; *Elegant Glassware of the Depression Era*, in its fourth edition; *The Collector's Encyclopedia of Akro Agate*; *The Collector's Encyclopedia of Occupied Japan*, Volumes I, II, III and IV; *Very Rare Glassware of the Depression Years* , Volumes I and II; and the *Pocket Guide to Depression Glass,* now in its seventh edition. He recently completed the fourth edition of his innovative *Standard Baseball Card Price Guide* which has been very well received in those circles.

Should you be in Lexington, he is sometimes found at Grannie Bear Antique Shop located at 120 Clay Avenue. The shop (site of his mother's former day care business) derived its name from the term of endearment toddlers gave her. In recent days he has been spending most of his time in Florida where his writing is an easier task without the phone ringing every five minutes — and fishing is just a cast away!

If you know of any unlisted or unusual pieces of glassware in the **patterns shown in this book,** you may write him May-October at Box 22186, Lexington, KY 40522, and November-April at Box 64, Astatula, FL 34705. If you expect a reply, you must enclose a SASE (self-addressed, stamped envelope) - and be patient. His writing, research and travels often cause the hundreds of letters he receives weekly to backlog. He appreciates your interest, however, and spends many hours answering your letters when time and circumstances permit. Remember that SASE! He does not open all that mail. Most letters without SASE are never read by him!

On The Cover: Beaded Edge cup & saucer $15.00; Holiday 4" footed juice $10.00; Fire-King Jane Ray creamer $4.00; Jamestown pitcher $110.00; and Bubble stemware goblet $11.50. Moroccan Amethyst octagonal fruit bowl $9.00; Fire King Game Bird mug $7.50; Yellow Moderntone sherbet $4.00; Green Sandwich juice tumbler $3.50.

Additional copies of this book may be ordered from:

COLLECTOR BOOKS
P.O. Box 3009
Paducah, Kentucky 42002-3009

or

GENE FLORENCE

(May 1- Oct. 31)   (Nov. 1- April 30)
P.O. Box 22186   P.O. Box 64
Lexington, KY 40522   Astatula, FL 34705

@$19.95. Add $2.00 for postage and handling.

ACKNOWLEDGMENTS

Thanks to all you readers and people at shows who kept me informed with your letters, cards and reports of new information! All this knowledge overcrowded my Collector's Encyclopedia of Depression Glass to the point that there was no more room to add new patterns or information! Too, as time has progressed, more and more patterns made **after** the Depression era are being collected; all this started me thinking about this book *Collectible Glassware from the 1940's, 1950's, 1960's....* It's taken five years; but one benefit of the procedure is now, Lord willing, there's room in both books for expansion!

A special thanks to all the glass clubs and show promoters who have invited me to their shows. Many of these shows are conducting seminars to increase collecting knowledge. This is a valuable trend if not overdone. It has increased attendance at shows - and hopefully, collector's knowledge of glassware!

A special thanks to Cathy, my wife, who, over twenty years of writing, has become chief editor and critic. She still tries to make sense out of my run-on or "non" sentences. (I know what I mean!) It has been particularly hard when I have been writing in Florida and she is editing in Kentucky. We definitely will see that "being in two places at one time" change with Marc, my youngest son, entering college about the time this book becomes available.

A special thanks to "Grannie Bear," my Mom, who spent hours wrapping and packing glass for the numerous photography sessions we had for this book. She has done an admirable job keeping glass separated for all the different categories: Elegant, Depression, 1950's and Kitchenware. Too, she's provided valuable input on pricing and children's dishes.

Thanks, too, to Cathy's Mom, Sibyl, who helped Cathy sort and pack glass for days and days! My gratitude to Dad, Charles, Sibyl and Marc who kept everything under control at home while we travelled. Now that Chad has moved out on his own, Marc has had to take over in his absence.

Glass and pricing information for this book were furnished by collectors and dealers from all over the country. These include: from Illinois, Dick and Pat Spencer, Dan Kramer; from Missouri, Gary and Sue Clark; from Ohio, Sam and Becky Collings, Dan Tucker and Lorrie Kitchen, Ralph Leslie, Jim Kennon and Phillip Bee of Anchor Hocking; from Washington, Carrie Domitz; from West Virginia, Frank Fenton of Fenton Art Glass; from Minnesota, Kaye Wahl; from Massachusetts, John Benkowski; from Alabama, Kathryn Forest; from Georgia, Bobby James; from Tennessee, Jimmy Gilbreath; from Kentucky, Jackie Morgan, Gwen Key, Gladys and Gene Florence, Sr., Debbie Summers and Beth Summers. Additional information came from numerous readers from across the U.S.A., Canada, England, Puerto Rico, New Zealand and Australia! Yes, there are avid collectors "down under!" Please know I am grateful to one and all!

A very special thanks to Michelle Fredrickson of Miki's Crystal Registry, P.O. Box 22506GF, Robbinsdale, MN 55422, for much of the Fostoria catalogue information in this book. She operates a Fostoria matching service if you are searching for any pieces.

Photographs for the book were made at Curtis and Mays Studio in Paducah by Tom Clouser. Glass arranging, unpacking, sorting, carting and repacking was accomplished by Dick Spencer, Steve Quertermous, Jane White, Lisa Stroup and Cathy Florence. No one walks away from helping at these sessions without wondering if we are not completely out of our minds for doing this. The employees at the photography studio greet us with "Not you again!" You could not believe what we go through to get you these photographs for your viewing pleasure. Sometimes the glass is hauled to Paducah (260 miles) as many as three times to get it right.

Thanks for the measurements and the photographs confirming new discoveries! Those photographs are invaluable when confirming pieces. If you have trouble photographing glass, take it outside in natural light, place the glass on a neutral surface and forget the camera has a flash attachment. A cloudy bright day works best. Please enclose SASE (self addressed stamped envelope) that is large enough to send back your pictures, if you wish them returned! Oft times the SASE to send back the pictures has been smaller than the photographs.

Thanks to the special people in the Editing Department at Collector Books: Steve Quertermous, Jane White, Della Maze, Beth Ray and Lisa Stroup. It was a farewell performance from Jane and Steve who have helped on my books for about fifteen years. Both helped in arranging our set-ups for photography sessions and they will be missed! Jane will still be working independently, but Steve has started his own business with his brother. I know he will miss my phone calls after work when there are problems! Good luck to both in your new endeavors!

FOREWORD

Starting a new book is quite an experience. It took at least five years of planning to make this book a reality. When the eighth *Collector's Encyclopedia of Depression Glass* was being written, I found that there was no room to expand to other patterns without going over my 224 page limitation which we hold to try and keep the price of the book down for you, the consumer. What I realized was that there were more and more patterns that were made after the Depression era being collected by Depression glass enthusiasts. I had an idea that is now this book. That idea has gone through transitions from the initial concept; but basically, this book covers glassware made after the Depression era allowing me to expand my other book by removing non-Depression era glassware. All patterns included in this book that were removed from *Collector's Encyclopedia of Depression Glass* will also be in that tenth edition as their swan song. Next time, the patterns made 1940 and after will be found only in this book.

I am including both mass produced and handmade glassware from this era since both types are avidly sought. Some of the glassware patterns included were started near the end of the 1930's, but the main production of these few patterns was the 1940's, 1950's or even later.

Fire-King and Anniversary have always been considered Depression Glass, but neither pattern was introduced until the 1940's. I have spent considerable time compiling available information on Fire-King lines. These are only examples of some of patterns included herein; there are many more.

Fenton has been a company that had few dinnerware lines introduced before 1940, so I have included some of their lines.

I have also included company catalogue pages of many of the patterns shown in this book. Let me know whether you like this or not. I have always felt that the glass itself is more important; but if you enjoy the catalogue pages, please let me know for the second edition. I felt it important at this juncture of a new book to include proof of research done.

Take a look at this beginning book, and let me know what additional patterns you would like to see included in the next edition. I have only scratched the surface of this vast time period, but it is a start! If you have collections from this time period, you'd be willing to lend for photography purposes or copies of glass company advertisements you received with your sets listing pieces, let me hear from you about those.

Collectors' demand and collecting habits will determine the direction the book will take in the future. This is my answer to the present direction I see collectors taking. It will probably take a couple of editions to make this book's format standard. I hope you learn from it and enjoy it!

PRICING

ALL PRICES IN THIS BOOK ARE RETAIL PRICES FOR MINT CONDITION GLASSWARE. THIS BOOK IS INTENDED TO BE ONLY A GUIDE TO PRICES AS THERE ARE SOME REGIONAL PRICE DIFFERENCES WHICH CANNOT REASONABLY BE DEALT WITH HEREIN.

You may expect dealers to pay from forty to fifty percent less than the prices quoted. Glass that is in less than mint condition, i.e. chipped, cracked, scratched or poorly molded, will bring only a small percentage of the price of glass that is in mint condition. Since this book covers glassware made from 1940 onward, you may expect that collectors will be less tolerant of usage marks or wear than glass made earlier.

Prices are fairly well standardized due to national advertising carried by specialized antique publications and dealers who attend Antique Glass Shows held from coast to coast. However, there are still some regional differences in prices due partly to glass being more readily available in some areas than in others. Too, companies distributed certain pieces in some areas that they did not in others. Generally speaking, however, prices are about the same among dealers from coast to coast.

Prices tend to increase dramatically on rare items and, in general, they have increased as a whole due to more and more collectors entering the field (and people becoming more aware of the worth of Depression and 1950's Glass).

One of the more important aspects of this book is the attempt made to illustrate as well as realistically price those items which are in demand. The desire was to give you the most accurate guide to collectible glass patterns available.

MEASUREMENTS

All measurements are taken from actual company catalogues or by actually measuring each piece itself, if no catalogue lists were available. Tumblers, stemware and pitchers are always measured to the very top edge until nothing more can be added to it. Heights are measured perpendicular to the bottom of the piece, and not up a slanted side. Plate measurements were usually rounded to the nearest inch, across the widest point; and this creates problems, today, when we go for exactness!

TABLE OF CONTENTS

ANNIVERSARY JEANNETTE GLASS COMPANY, 1947-49; late 1960's - mid 1970's

Colors: pink, crystal, and iridescent.

While working on the Eighth edition of *The Collector's Encyclopedia of Depression Glass*, I realized that there was a need for a book that covered the glassware made beyond that era. It has taken five years to make that book a reality; here it begins, this time not with Adam, but with Anniversary!

Anniversary, though purchased by Depression Glass collectors, was never made during that time period thought of as the Depression era. Jeannette continued production of this pattern in crystal well into the 1970's. The heavily promoted iridized color made in the 1970's is beginning to be sought by collectors; but it was not made in as many pieces as were the other colors.

Pink was only listed in catalogues from 1947 until 1949; but crystal and iridized colors could be bought in boxed sets in "dish barn" outlets as late as 1975. I can still remember in the early 1970's, being offered about twenty boxed sets for only $10.00 each at Sam's Truck Stop in Georgetown, Kentucky, one of the first flea markets in my area. I didn't buy them then, but I might reconsider today! I now see more and more iridized Anniversary at flea markets, but little has been allowed into Depression era glass shows since it is considered to be too recently made. Iridescent is often priced and marked as if it were Carnival glass by unknowing "dealers," but it is actually fetching prices closer to those of pink Anniversary than that of crystal.

There is a steady demand for pink and now even the iridescent; and after years of little demand, prices for crystal Anniversary have finally begun to increase. Crystal is harder to find than other colors, as many new collectors have found out.

Items that are hardest to find include the butter dish, pin-up vase, candy dish, wine glass and sandwich plate. The bottom to the butter is harder to find than the top. This seems to hold true for many patterns which have heavy lids and flattened or thinner bottoms. I might add that there are several styles of aluminum lids found on the cake plate. No, I have no idea which is the "correct" one. The glass companies did not make these lids, but either bid them out or sold the bottoms to someone who made the tops by special order.

I still get letters about the word comport after all these years. The Jeannette catalog from 1947 lists the open, three-legged candy as a comport and not a compote. They mean the same thing. Terminology has simply changed over time.

	Crystal	Pink	Iridescent
Bowl, 4⅞", berry	2.50	6.00	4.00
Bowl, 7⅜", soup	6.00	12.50	6.50
Bowl, 9", fruit	9.00	17.50	10.00
Butter dish bottom	10.00	25.00	
Butter dish top	12.50	22.50	
Butter dish and cover	22.50	47.50	
Candy jar and cover	17.50	37.50	
Cake plate, 12½"	5.50	12.50	
Cake plate w/metal cover	12.00		
Candlestick, 4⅞" pr.	15.00		
Comport, open, 3 legged	3.50	9.00	4.50
Creamer, footed	3.50	8.50	5.00
Cup	2.50	6.50	3.75
Pickle dish, 9"	4.00	9.00	6.00
Plate, 6¼", sherbet	1.25	2.00	1.50
Plate, 9", dinner	4.00	8.00	5.75
Plate, 12½", sandwich server	4.00	10.00	7.50
Relish dish, 8"	4.50	8.50	6.00
Saucer	1.00	1.50	1.25
Sherbet, ftd.	2.50	6.50	
Sugar	2.00	6.00	4.00
Sugar cover	4.00	8.50	2.50
Tid-bit, berry & fruit bowls w/metal hndl.	12.00		
Vase, 6½"	12.00	25.00	
Vase, wall pin-up	12.00	22.50	
Wine glass, 2½ oz.	7.00	15.00	

Please refer to Foreword for pricing information

"BEADED EDGE" (PATTERN #22 MILK GLASS) WESTMORELAND GLASS COMPANY, late1930's-1950's

"Beaded Edge" is a collector's name for Westmoreland's Pattern #22 milk glass. There are eight different flowers and fruits on this pattern as well as plain white and a decorated red edge called Coral-Red by Westmoreland. The sherbets are harder to find than tumblers, plates, or cups and saucers; but the 12" platter and 15" torte plate are the key pieces to find according to several collectors I've talked with who have collected "Beaded Edge" for years. There is supposedly a three part relish to be found; but I have never seen one decorated.

The sugar and creamer shown here belong to another Westmoreland line (Pattern #108) and not Beaded Edge; but the fruit decorations make it a great item to go with the fruit decorated Beaded Edge, so we have included them here. While cherries are shown on the side that is pictured, blueberries are on the opposite side away from the camera. If you collect either one of these fruit patterns, I suggest you find a set of these Pattern #108 instead of the normally found footed ones. Note that these "patterns" were actually **numbers** and not the "names" that collectors are so fond of using. This is true of many company's glassware lines.

	Plain	Red Edge	Decorated
Creamer, ftd.	10.00	12.00	15.00
Creamer, ftd. w/lid #108	15.00	20.00	25.00
Cup	5.00	7.50	10.00
Nappy, 5"	4.00	6.00	9.00
Nappy, 6", crimped, oval	6.00	9.00	13.00
Plate, 6", bread and butter	4.00	6.00	9.00
Plate, 7", salad	6.00	9.00	12.00
Plate, 8½", luncheon	6.00	9.00	12.00
Plate, 10½", dinner	10.00	15.00	22.50
Plate, 15", torte	17.50	30.00	40.00
Platter, 12", oval w/tab hndls.	17.50	30.00	40.00
Relish, 3 part	20.00		
Salt and pepper, pr.	17.50	22.50	32.50
Saucer	2.00	3.00	5.00
Sherbet, ftd.	6.00	9.00	15.00
Sugar, ftd.	10.00	12.00	15.00
Sugar, ftd. w/lid #108	15.00	20.00	25.00
Tumbler, 8 oz., ftd.	7.00	10.00	15.00

"BUBBLE," "BULLSEYE," "PROVINCIAL" ANCHOR HOCKING GLASS COMPANY, 1940-1965

Colors: Pink, Sapphire blue, Forest Green, Royal Ruby, crystal and any known Hocking color.

Bubble is a pattern that introduces many beginners to collecting! Blue is usually the color that first attracts them because of the abundant supply of cups, saucers and dinner plates. All other pieces in blue seem to be found in lesser quantities, especially creamers which have always been in shorter supply than sugar bowls! The 9" flanged bowl has all but disappeared from the collecting scene. You can see this bowl on the right at the very back of the photo at the top of page 11. Fortunately, it is standing up so you can see the flanged rim to differentiate it from the regular berry bowl shown in the center of that photo.

Forest Green (dark) and Royal Ruby (red) continue to sell extremely well.

Pink is hard to find in any piece other than the 8⅜" bowl. I looked for that stack of pink bowls which I saw in one of my first trips to Hocking when I was there in December; but alas, I have never seen them again. On the West coast last week, I noticed a big price on this bowl; but in my area, they are a tough sale in the $5.00 range. The depth of these bowls vary.

That 8⅜" berry bowl can be found in almost any color that Anchor Hocking made since WWII (including all the opaque colors common to Hocking). Milk White was only listed in the 1959-60 catalogue.

I have included some Anchor Hocking color catalogue sheets throughout this book which I hope you will find enlightening. I call attention to these catalogue sheets to refer to some new items listed in the prices. On the bottom of page 12 notice some stemware that was sold along with Bubble. These have been called "Boopie" by collectors, but they are priced about the same as the "Bubble stemware" shown on page 15 with the Forest Green Bubble.

According to one Anchor Hocking catalogue, the Bubble stemware was actually called "Early American" line. Both these stemware lines come with Forest Green and Royal Ruby tops as well as an all crystal version. Most of my collectors of Bubble prefer the stems shown on page 15; but you officially have your choice of two styles to go with your dinnerware. Both of these were made after production of blue had ceased; so, there are no blue stems to be found. Sorry!

The catalogue lists an iced tea in "Boopie" with a capacity of 15 oz.; but all we have actually been able to put in one is 14 oz!

Note the iridized green sugar in the bottom picture. I still have not found a creamer to go with this. Opaque white, iridized and amber colors had to be short lived since so few of these colors have been seen. The odd blue cup in the top picture is one of several pieces found in that color in Texas. It appears to be Bubble, but is not a typical Hocking color.

The labels on the crystal Bubble read "Heat Proof." In fact, a 1942 ad guaranteed this "Fire-King" tableware to be "heat-proof," indeed a "tableware that can be used in the oven, on the table, in the refrigerator." Presumably since this ad is dated 1942, they're referring to the light blue color. This added dimension is unique to "Fire-King" since most Depression glass patterns will not hold up to sudden changes in temperature.

	Crystal	Forest Green	Light Blue	Royal Ruby
Bowl, 4", berry	2.50		12.00	
Bowl, 4½", fruit	3.50	5.50	9.00	7.50
Bowl, 5¼", cereal	4.00	9.50	10.00	
Bowl, 7¾", flat soup	4.50		12.00	
Bowl, 8⅜", large berry (Pink-$6.00)	5.50	11.00	14.00	15.00
Bowl, 9", flanged			175.00	
Candlesticks, pr.	12.50	22.50		
Creamer	4.50	9.50	27.50	
*Cup	3.00	5.00	3.00	4.50
Lamp, 3 styles	37.50			
Pitcher, 64 oz., ice lip	55.00			45.00
Plate, 6¾", bread and butter	1.50	3..00	3.00	
Plate, 9⅜", grill			17.50	
Plate, 9⅜", dinner	4.00	12.50	6.00	8.00
Platter, 12", oval	7.50		14.00	
**Saucer	1.00	3.00	1.50	3.00
***Stem, 3½ oz., cocktail	3.50	7.00		8.00

	Crystal	Forest Green	Light Blue	Royal Ruby
***Stem, 4 oz., juice	4.00	9.00		10.00
Stem, 4½ oz., cocktail	4.00	8.00		9.00
Stem, 5½ oz., juice	5.00	10.00		11.00
***Stem, 6 oz., sherbet	3.00	7.00		8.00
Stem, 6 oz., sherbet	3.50	7.50		8.50
***Stem, 9 oz., goblet	7.00	12.00		12.50
Stem, 9½ oz., goblet	6.00	11.00		11.50
***Stem, 14 oz., iced tea	7.00	17.50		
Sugar	4.50	9.00	15.00	
Tidbit (2 tier)				30.00
Tumbler, 6 oz., juice	3.50			7.00
Tumbler, 8 oz., 3¼", old fashioned	6.00			15.00
Tumbler, 9 oz., water	5.00			8.00
Tumbler, 12 oz., 4½", iced tea	7.00			10.00
Tumbler, 16 oz., 5⅞", lemonade	9.00			16.00

*Pink - $75.00
**Pink - $25.00
***"Boopie"

Please refer to Foreword for pricing information

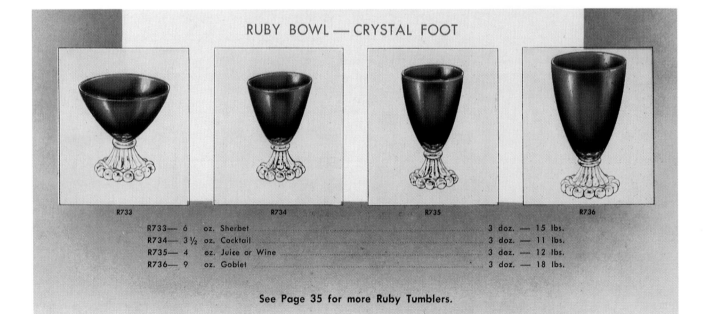

RUBY BOWL — CRYSTAL FOOT

R733	R734	R735	R736

R733— 6 oz. Sherbet .... 3 doz. — 15 lbs.
R734— 3½ oz. Cocktail .... 3 doz. — 11 lbs.
R735— 4 oz. Juice or Wine .... 3 doz. — 12 lbs.
R736— 9 oz. Goblet .... 3 doz. — 18 lbs.

See Page 35 for more Ruby Tumblers.

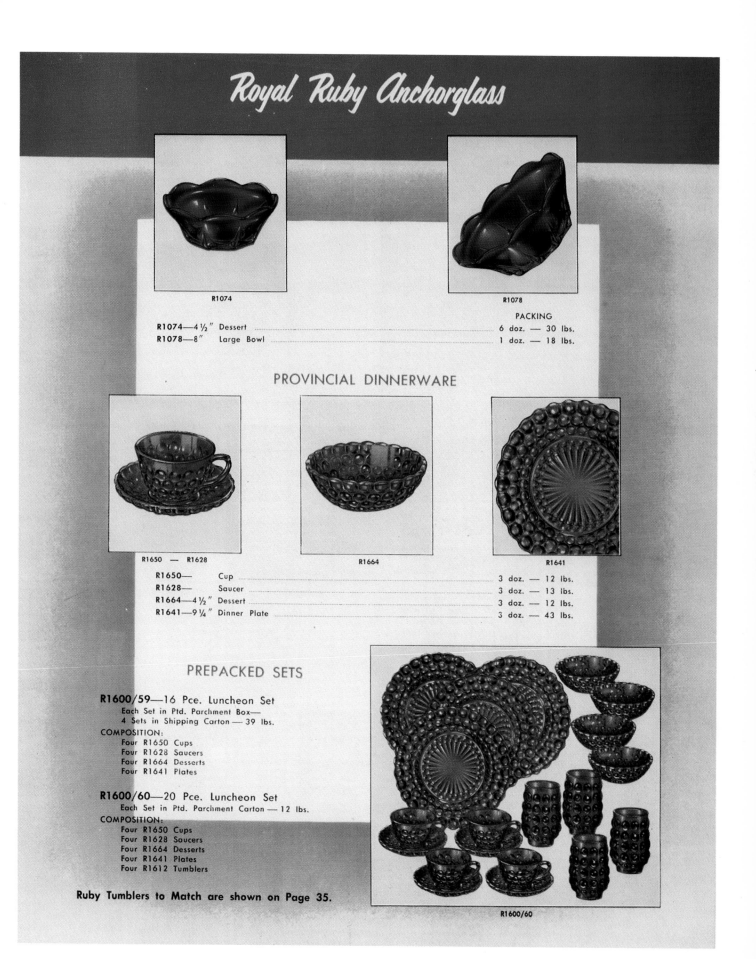

Royal Ruby Anchorglass

R1074

R1078

		PACKING
R1074—4½"	Dessert	6 doz. — 30 lbs.
R1078—8"	Large Bowl	1 doz. — 18 lbs.

PROVINCIAL DINNERWARE

R1650 — R1628

R1664

R1641

R1650—	Cup	3 doz. — 12 lbs.
R1628—	Saucer	3 doz. — 13 lbs.
R1664—4½"	Dessert	3 doz. — 12 lbs.
R1641—9¼"	Dinner Plate	3 doz. — 43 lbs.

PREPACKED SETS

R1600/59—16 Pce. Luncheon Set
Each Set in Ptd. Parchment Box—
4 Sets in Shipping Carton — 39 lbs.
COMPOSITION:
    Four R1650 Cups
    Four R1628 Saucers
    Four R1664 Desserts
    Four R1641 Plates

R1600/60—20 Pce. Luncheon Set
Each Set in Ptd. Parchment Carton — 12 lbs.
COMPOSITION:
    Four R1650 Cups
    Four R1628 Saucers
    Four R1664 Desserts
    Four R1641 Plates
    Four R1612 Tumblers

Ruby Tumblers to Match are shown on Page 35.

R1600/60

13

Royal Ruby "Provincial" Tumblers

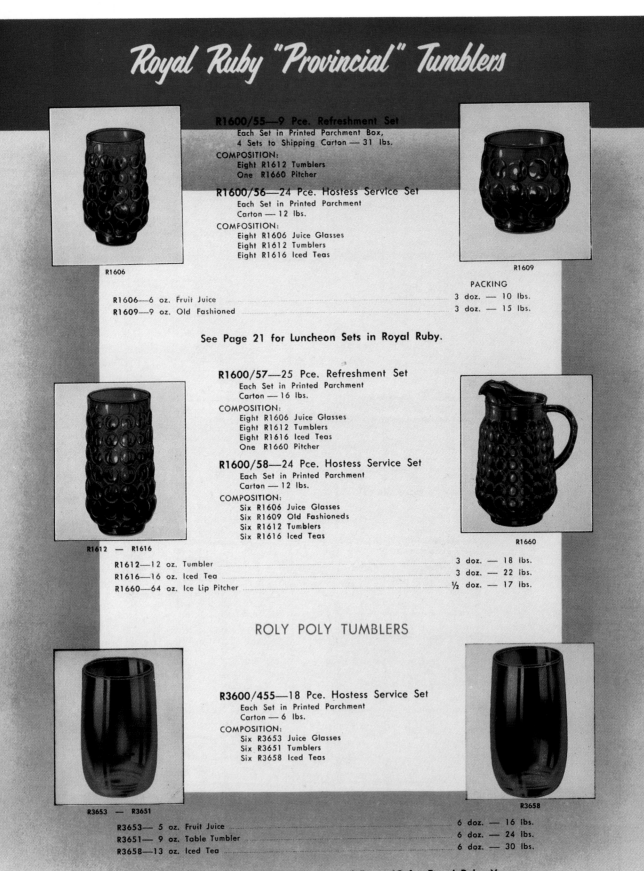

R1600/55—9 Pce. Refreshment Set
Each Set in Printed Parchment Box,
4 Sets to Shipping Carton — 31 lbs.
COMPOSITION:
    Eight R1612 Tumblers
    One R1660 Pitcher

R1600/56—24 Pce. Hostess Service Set
Each Set in Printed Parchment
Carton — 12 lbs.
COMPOSITION:
    Eight R1606 Juice Glasses
    Eight R1612 Tumblers
    Eight R1616 Iced Teas

R1606

R1609

PACKING

R1606—6 oz. Fruit Juice	3 doz. —	10 lbs.
R1609—9 oz. Old Fashioned	3 doz. —	15 lbs.

See Page 21 for Luncheon Sets in Royal Ruby.

R1600/57—25 Pce. Refreshment Set
Each Set in Printed Parchment
Carton — 16 lbs.
COMPOSITION:
    Eight R1606 Juice Glasses
    Eight R1612 Tumblers
    Eight R1616 Iced Teas
    One R1660 Pitcher

R1600/58—24 Pce. Hostess Service Set
Each Set in Printed Parchment
Carton — 12 lbs.
COMPOSITION:
    Six R1606 Juice Glasses
    Six R1609 Old Fashioneds
    Six R1612 Tumblers
    Six R1616 Iced Teas

R1612 — R1616

R1660

R1612—12 oz. Tumbler	3 doz. —	18 lbs.
R1616—16 oz. Iced Tea	3 doz. —	22 lbs.
R1660—64 oz. Ice Lip Pitcher	½ doz. —	17 lbs.

ROLY POLY TUMBLERS

R3600/455—18 Pce. Hostess Service Set
Each Set in Printed Parchment
Carton — 6 lbs.
COMPOSITION:
    Six R3653 Juice Glasses
    Six R3651 Tumblers
    Six R3658 Iced Teas

R3653 — R3651

R3658

R3653— 5 oz. Fruit Juice	6 doz. —	16 lbs.
R3651— 9 oz. Table Tumbler	6 doz. —	24 lbs.
R3658—13 oz. Iced Tea	6 doz. —	30 lbs.

See Page 67 for Royal Ruby Ash Trays and Page 69 for Royal Ruby Vases.

FOREST GREEN Anchorglass®
Dinnerware

E1600/46—22 PCE. LUNCHEON SET
Each Set in Gift Ctn., 4 Sets to Shipping Ctn.—50 lbs.
COMPOSITION:
Four E1650 Cups   Four E336 Goblets
Four E1628 Saucers   One E1653 Sugar
Four E1665 Cereals   One E1654 Creamer
Four E1641 Dinner Plates

E1600/45—18 PCE. LUNCHEON SET
Each Set in Gift Ctn., 4 Sets
to Shipping Ctn.—42 lbs.
COMPOSITION:
Four E1650 Cups   Four E1641-9¼" Plates
Four E1628 Saucers   One E1653 Sugar
Four E1665 Cereals   One E1654 Creamer

E1600/47—30 PCE. LUNCHEON SET
Each Set in Shipping Ctn.—22 lbs.
COMPOSITION:
Four E1650 Cups   Four E336 Goblets
Four E1628 Saucers   Four E333 Sherbets
Four E1665 Cereals   One E1653 Sugar
Four E1630-6⅜" Plates   One E1654 Creamer
Four E1641-9¼" Plates

E1650—8 OZ. CUP
Pkd. 6 doz.—22 lbs.

E1628—5¾" SAUCER
Pkd. 6 doz.—24 lbs.

E1665—5¼" CEREAL
Pkd. 6 doz.—35 lbs.

E1630—6⅝" PIE OR
SALAD PLATE
Pkd. 6 doz.—38 lbs.

E1641—9¼" DINNER
PLATE
Pkd. 3 doz.—38 lbs.

FOREST GREEN AND CRYSTAL STEMWARE

E336—9½ OZ. GOBLET
Pkd. 3 doz.—17 lbs.

E335—5½ OZ. F. JUICE
Pkd. 3 doz.—10 lbs.

E334—4½ OZ. COCKTAIL
Pkd. 3 doz.—9 lbs.

E333—6 OZ. SHERBET
Pkd. 3 doz.—16 lbs.

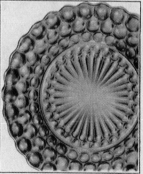

E1653—FOOTED
SUGAR
Pkd. 3 doz.—18 lbs.

E1654—FOOTED
CREAMER
Pkd. 3 doz.—18 lbs.

E300/174—8 PCE. GOBLET SET
8 Pieces in Gift Ctn.—
6 Sets to Shipping Ctn.—26 lbs.
COMP.: Eight E336 Goblets

E300/175—8 PCE. JUICE SET
8 Pieces in Gift Ctn.—
6 Sets to Shipping Ctn.—15 lbs.
COMP.: Eight E335 Juice Glasses

E300/176—8 PCE. COCKTAIL SET
8 Pieces in Gift Ctn.—
6 Sets to Shipping Ctn.—15 lbs.
COMP.: Eight E334 Cocktails

E300/177—8 PCE. SHERBET SET
8 Pieces in Gift Ctn.—
6 Sets to Shipping Ctn.—24 lbs.
COMP.: Eight E333 Sherbets

CABOCHON A.H. HEISEY & COMPANY, 1950-1957

Colors: amber, crystal and Dawn.

Cabochon is one of the lesser known 1950's Heisey patterns outside the world of Heisey collectors. Although there are a few pieces found in amber and Dawn, Cabochon is mostly found in crystal. Prices are reasonable for this pattern which was made near the end of the Heisey company's closing in 1957. This listing is taken from a 1953 catalogue.

The tumbler listed as 5 oz., juice, ftd., #6091 looks more like a parfait than a juice tumbler.

Colored pieces of Cabochon will be priced in the next edition.

	Crystal		Crystal
Bon bon, 6¼", hndl.,		Relish, 9", three part, oblong #1951	17.50
(sides sloped w/squared hndl.) #1951	20.00	Relish, 9", three part, square #1951	15.00
Bottle, oil, w/#101 stopper #1951	25.00	Salt and pepper, square, w/#60 silver	
Bowl, 4½", dessert #1951	3.00	plated tops, pr. #1951	10.00
Bowl, 5", dessert #1951	3.50	Saucer #1951	1.00
Bowl, 7", cereal #1951	5.00	Sherbet, 6 oz. #1951 (pressed)	3.00
Bowl, 13", floral or salad #1951	15.00	Sherbet, 6 oz. #6092 (blown)	3.00
Bowl, 13", gardenia		Stemware, 1 oz., cordial #6091	12.00
(low w/edge cupped irregularly) #1951	15.00	Stemware, 3 oz., oyster cocktail #6091	3.00
Butter dish, ¼ lb. #1951	22.50	Stemware, 3 oz., wine #6091	7.00
Cake salver, ftd. #1951	60.00	Stemware, 4 oz., cocktail #6091	3.00
Candle holder, 2 lite, ground bottom, pr. #1951	125.00	Stemware, 5½ oz., sherbet #6091	3.00
Candlette, 1 lite (like bowl), pr. #1951	50.00	Stemware, 10 oz., goblet #6091	7.00
Candy, 6¼", w/lid (bowl w/lid) #1951	27.50	Sugar, w/cover #1951	12.50
Cheese, 5¾", ftd., compote for cracker plate	15.00	Tidbit, 7½" (bowl w/sloped outsides) #1951	10.00
Cream #1951	8.00	Tray, 9", for cream and sugar #1951	35.00
Creamer, cereal, 12 oz. #1951	25.00	Tumbler, 5 oz. #1951 (pressed)	5.00
Cup #1951	5.00	Tumbler, 5 oz., juice, flat bottomed #6092 (blown)	5.00
Jelly, 6", hndl., (sides and hndl. rounded) #1951	20.00	Tumbler, 5 oz., juice, ftd. #6091	6.00
Mayonnaise, 3 pc. (plate, bowl, ladle) #1951	22.50	Tumbler, 10 oz., beverage #6092 (blown)	7.00
Mint, 5¾", ftd., (sides slanted) #1951	20.00	Tumbler, 10 oz., tumbler #6092 (blown)	7.00
Pickle tray, 8½" #1951	18.00	Tumbler, 12 oz. #1951 (pressed)	10.00
Plate, 8", salad #1951	5.00	Tumbler, 12 oz., ice tea #6092 (blown)	12.00
Plate, 13", center hndl. #1951	35.00	Tumbler, 12 oz., ice tea, ftd. #6091	7.00
Plate, 14", cracker w/center ring #1951	15.00	Tumbler, 14 oz., soda #6092 (blown)	9.00
Plate, 14", party (edge cupped irregularly) #1951	15.00	Vase, 3½", flared #1951	15.00
Plate, 14", sandwich #1951	15.00		

CAPRI HAZEL WARE, DIVISION OF CONTINENTAL CAN, 1960's

Color: azure blue.

The name "Capri" probably refers to the color of this ware rather than the pattern. I base this conjecture on the fact that their purple color called Moroccan Amethyst encompassed several separate patterns. (Hazel Ware, by the way, had previously been called Hazel Atlas before being bought out by Continental Can). I have found no catalogue showing this pattern, but many labelled pieces are being found that say **CAPRI**; so that is what we will call this pattern until otherwise identified. Several dealers have been stocking Capri after I mentioned it in my previous edition of *The Collector's Encyclopedia of Depression Glass* when writing about the Moroccan Amethyst. I mentioned that many of these same pieces also come in crystal; however, no one has written to say that they have found a label to identify a name for the crystal. Let me know if you find one!

I suspect that the blue color of this pattern will make it highly collectible in the near future. Since Capri is now approaching thirty years since production, more and more pieces will be finding their way out of homes through garage, tag and estate sales. It seems to take about twenty to thirty years to create a secondary market of a limited production pattern. If a pattern were widely distributed, then it does not take as long for people to start looking for items to complete sets that were never finished when the pattern was being made.

The candy dish used as a pattern shot on the next page and the two swirled bowls are some of the few items that are also not found in Moroccan Amethyst, or at least, I have not found either. I originally thought that all pieces found in blue would be the same shape as Moroccan Amethyst, but that has not been the case.

From a reader I recently received a group of photographs of many unknown pieces of Capri, i.e. round cups, saucers, plates and even a creamer and sugar that had been found in Alabama. Plates have circular dots leading to an open center. Hopefully, I will have one to show you by the next edition. The stems found in Alabama have hexagonal bases and the tumblers are square or pentagonal. All these pieces have labels; so this adds further credence to Capri being the color's name.

Keep looking! I am sure there are more pieces awaiting discovery!

	Blue		Blue
Ash tray, ¾", triangular	5.00	Plate, 5¾", bread and butter, octagonal	4.00
Ash tray, 3¼", round	5.00	Plate, 7⅛", salad, round	6.50
Ash tray, 6⅞", triangular	10.00	Plate, 7¼", salad, octagonal	6.50
Bowl, 4¾", octagonal	6.50	Plate, 9⅞", dinner, round	8.00
Bowl, 4¾", swirled	7.50	Plate, 9¾", dinner, octagonal	8.00
Bowl, 5⅜", salad, round	5.50	Plate, 10", snack, fan shaped w/cup rest	7.00
Bowl, 5¾", square, deep	9.00	Saucer, 6", round	2.00
Bowl, 6"	7.00	Saucer, octagonal	2.00
Bowl, 7¾", oval	15.00	Stem, 4½", sherbet	6.00
Bowl, 7¾", rectangular	15.00	Stem, 5½", water	8.00
Bowl, 8¾", swirled	17.50	Sugar w/lid, round	10.00
Bowl, 10¾", salad	22.50	Tid bit, 3 tier	
Candy jar, w/cover, ftd.	25.00	(round 9⅞" plate, 7⅛" plate, 6" saucer)	20.00
Chip and dip, 2 swirled bowls		Tumbler, 3", fruit	4.00
(8¾" and 4¾" on metal rack)	30.00	Tumbler, 3¼", old fashioned	7.50
Creamer, round	7.50	Tumbler, 4¼", water	6.50
Cup, octagonal	5.00	Tumbler, 5", tea	8.50
Cup, round	5.00	Vase, 8½", ruffled	27.50

CENTURY, LINE #2630, FOSTORIA GLASS COMPANY

Color: crystal.

"Stemware in the Century pattern have some big prices on the West Coast!" I made that statement in my fourth edition of *Elegant Glassware of the Depression Era* and the prices in the East went up! In particular wines and footed iced teas have increased about fifty percent which makes prices more in line with those in the West. However, on a whole in the west, prices for Elegant glassware are more reasonable than the prices for Depression glassware. I have just returned from Eugene, Oregon, and dealers are having a difficult time stocking basic patterns, serving pieces in particular.

There are two sizes of dinner plates as is the case in most of Fostoria's patterns. The larger plate is the harder to find. They were priced higher originally, and many people did without the larger plates. Prices below are for mint (not scratched or worn) plates.

The ice bucket has a metal handle and tabs for the handle to attach. An 8½" oval vase shaped like the ice bucket without these "tabs" is often mistaken for an ice tub. This vase is shown in the top picture on the right side in the back.

There is still some confusion between the candy and the covered preserve. The candy w/cover stands 7" tall, but the preserve w/cover only stands 6" tall and has a stemmed bottom. The candy is shown in the bottom photo.

	Crystal		Crystal
Ashtray, 2¾"	9.00	Pitcher, 7⅛", 48 oz.	90.00
Basket, 10¼" x 6½", wicker hndl.	65.00	Plate, 6½", bread/butter	5.00
Bowl, 4½", hndl.	11.00	Plate, 7½", salad	7.50
Bowl, 5", fruit	12.50	Plate, 7½", crescent salad	32.50
Bowl, 6", cereal	20.00	Plate, 8", party, w/indent for cup	20.00
Bowl, 6¼", snack, ftd.	12.50	Plate, 8½", luncheon	12.00
Bowl, 7⅛", 3 ftd., triangular	14.00	Plate, 9½", small dinner	20.00
Bowl, 7¼", bonbon, 3 ftd.	18.00	Plate, 10", hndl., cake	18.00
Bowl, 8", flared	22.00	Plate, 10½", dinner	27.50
Bowl, 8½", salad	22.00	Plate, 14", torte	27.50
Bowl, 9", lily pond	25.00	Platter, 12"	45.00
Bowl, 9½", hndl., serving bowl	25.00	Preserve, w/cover, 6"	30.00
Bowl, 9½", oval, serving bowl	30.00	Relish, 7⅜", 2 part	14.50
Bowl, 10", oval, hndl.	25.00	Relish, 11⅛", 3 part	20.00
Bowl, 10½", salad	25.00	Salt and pepper, 2⅜", individual, pr.	12.50
Bowl, 10¾", ftd., flared	27.50	Salt and pepper, 3⅛", pr.	17.50
Bowl, 11, ftd., rolled edge	37.50	Salver, 12¼", ftd. (like cake stand)	45.00
Bowl, 11¼", lily pond	30.00	Saucer	3.50
Bowl, 12", flared	30.00	Stem, 3½ oz., cocktail, 4⅛"	18.00
Butter, w/cover, ¼ lb.	30.00	Stem, 3½ oz., wine, 4½"	27.50
Candy, w/cover, 7"	32.50	Stem, 4½ oz., oyster cocktail, 3¾"	19.00
Candlestick, 4½"	15.00	Stem, 5½" oz., sherbet, 4½"	11.00
Candlestick, 7", double	27.50	Stem, 10 oz., goblet, 5¾"	20.00
Candlestick, 7¾", triple	35.00	Sugar, 4", ftd.	8.00
Comport, 2¾", cheese	15.00	Sugar, individual	8.00
Comport, 4⅜"	17.50	Tid bit, 8⅛", 3 ftd., upturned edge	17.50
Cracker plate, 10¾"	30.00	Tid bit, 10¼", 2 tier, metal hndl.	22.50
Creamer, 4¼"	8.00	Tray, 4¼", for ind. salt/pepper	12.50
Creamer, individual	8.00	Tray, 7⅛", for ind. sugar/creamer	12.00
Cup, 6 oz., ftd.	14.00	Tray, 9⅛", hndl., utility	22.00
Ice Bucket	55.00	Tray, 9½", hndl., muffin	25.00
Mayonnaise, 3 pc.	27.50	Tray, 11½", center hndl.	27.50
Mayonnaise, 4 pc., div. w/2 ladles	32.50	Tumbler, 5 oz., ftd., juice, 4¾"	20.00
Mustard, w/spoon, cover	25.00	Tumbler, 12 oz., ftd., tea, 5⅞"	25.00
Oil, w/stopper, 5 oz.	40.00	Vase, 6", bud	17.50
Pickle, 8¾"	13.50	Vase, 7½", hndl.	65.00
Pitcher, 6⅛", 16 oz.	45.00	Vase, 8½", oval	60.00

Please refer to Foreword for pricing information

CHINTZ, (PLATE ETCHING #338), FOSTORIA GLASS COMPANY

Color: crystal.

   The fact that Fostoria's Chintz was selling as well as Cambridge's Rose Point was news to me a couple of years ago! Since I find very little of it in my area except for stemware, I honestly found it hard to believe until I bought several large accumulations. I am convinced that it does sell as well!

   There are several new listings added since the fourth *Elegant Glassware of the Depression Era* was printed, thanks to a reader who sent me a jewelry store brochure. The metal drip cut syrup was listed as Sani-cut, so I have changed that to agree.

   That oval divided bowl on the left in the bottom photograph is the divided sauce boat. That piece also comes undivided. The sauce boat liner comes with both, but the brochure lists it as a tray instead of liner. Note that many pieces of Chintz pattern are found on the #2496 blank (known as Baroque).

   Crystal vases in etched Fostoria patterns are hard to find, so keep a lookout in your travels. Prices for dinner plates are for mint condition (no scratches or worn areas)!

	Crystal		Crystal
Bell, dinner	75.00	Plate, #2496, 10½", hndl., cake	40.00
Bowl, #869, 4½", finger	35.00	Plate, #2496, 11", cracker	39.50
Bowl, #2496, 4⅝", tri-cornered	20.00	Plate, #2496, 14", upturned edge	47.50
Bowl, #2496, 5", fruit	25.00	Plate, #2496, 16", torte, plain edge	95.00
Bowl, #2496, 5", hndl.	22.50	Platter, #2496, 12"	85.00
Bowl, #2496, 7⅝", bon bon	30.00	Relish, #2496, 6", 2 part, square	29.00
Bowl, #2496, 8½", hndl.	47.50	Relish, #2496, 10" x 7½", 3 part	37.50
Bowl, #2496, 9½", vegetable	65.00	Relish, #2419, 5 part	37.50
Bowl, #2484, 10", hndl.	55.00	Salad dressing bottle, #2083, 6½"	265.00
Bowl, #2496, 10½", hndl.	60.00	Salt and pepper, #2496, 2¾", flat, pr.	85.00
Bowl, #2496, 11½", flared	55.00	Sauce boat, #2496, oval	67.50
Bowl, #6023, ftd.	35.00	Sauce boat, #2496, oval, divided	62.50
Candlestick, #2496, 3½", double	27.50	Sauce boat liner, #2496, oblong, 8"	27.50
Candlestick, #2496, 4"	15.00	Saucer, #2496	5.00
Candlestick, #2496, 5½"	27.50	Stem, #6026, 1 oz., cordial, 3⅞"	42.50
Candlestick, #2496, 6", triple	39.50	Stem, #6026, 4 oz., cocktail, 5"	24.50
Candlestick, #6023, double	32.50	Stem, #6026, 4 oz., oyster cocktail, 3⅜"	25.00
Candy, w/cover, #2496, 3 part	100.00	Stem, #6026, 4½ oz., claret-wine, 5⅜"	37.50
Celery, #2496, 11"	32.50	Stem, #6026, 6 oz., low sherbet, 4⅜"	19.00
Comport, #2496, 3¼", cheese	22.50	Stem, #6026, 6 oz., saucer champagne, 5½"	19.50
Comport, #2496, 4¾"	30.00	Stem, #6026, 9 oz., water goblet, 7⅝"	29.50
Comport, #2496, 5½"	32.50	Sugar, #2496, 3½", ftd.	15.00
Creamer, #2496, 3¾", ftd.	16.00	Sugar, #2496½, individual	20.00
Creamer, #2496½, individual	20.00	Syrup, #2586 Sani-cut	300.00
Cup, #2496, ftd.	20.00	Tid bit, #2496, 8¼", 3 ftd., upturned edge	25.00
Ice bucket, #2496	115.00	Tray, #2496½, 6½", for ind. sugar/creamer	20.00
Jelly, w/cover, #2496, 7½"	80.00	Tray, #2375, 11", center hndl.	37.50
Mayonnaise, #2496½, 3 piece	55.00	Tumbler, #6026, 5 oz., juice, ftd.	24.50
Oil, w/stopper, #2496, 3½ oz.	90.00	Tumbler, #6026, 9 oz., water or low goblet	25.00
Pickle, #2496, 8"	29.50	Tumbler, #6026, 13 oz., tea, ftd.	29.50
Pitcher, #5000, 48 oz., ftd.	325.00	Vase, #4108, 5"	75.00
Plate, #2496, 6", bread/butter	9.00	Vase, #4128, 5"	75.00
Plate, #2496, 7½", salad	14.00	Vase, #4143, 6", ftd.	85.00
Plate, #2496, 8½", luncheon	20.00	Vase, #4143, 7½", ftd.	125.00
Plate, #2496, 9½", dinner	42.50		

Please refer to Foreword for pricing information

"CHRISTMAS CANDY," NO. 624 INDIANA GLASS COMPANY, 1950's

Colors: Terrace Green and crystal.

Christmas Candy is one of Indiana's numbered lines (#624), and almost all the pieces I have purchased over the years have come from trips into Indiana. It may have been only regionally distributed. Dunkirk, the home of Indiana Glass, is not far from Indianapolis where I attend several Depression glass shows each year.

Actually, a new piece of Christmas Candy has been found. You might expect that the newly discovered vegetable bowl would be found in Indiana and be brought to the Indianapolis Depression Glass show. In fact, the spring show is going on as I write this from my office in Florida. It is the first Indy show I have missed in a long time, but sometimes other things are more important! This book fits into the latter category; and if you don't believe it, just ask Collector Books!

Crystal Christmas Candy has few collectors, but it is a pattern that can still be found at reasonable prices. Some of the pieces of teal are no longer "reasonably priced" as you can see below.

Teal, or "Terrace Green" as it was named by the company, is the color everyone wants. Unfortunately, there is very little of this color found today. Usually, Christmas Candy is found in sets rather than a piece here and there. Any glassware made in the 1950's is often found in sets.

I had a report of a crystal small berry bowl, but no measurements or picture were included in the letter. However, I did get a letter about the following written on a boxed 15 piece set: "15 pc. Luncheon set (Terrace Green) To F W Newburger & Co. New Albany Ind Dept M 1346; From Pitman Dretzer Dunkirk Ind 4-3-52." The writer did not say if the glass were in the box, but it was valuable with its dated information.

	Crystal	Teal
Bowl, 7⅜", soup	6.00	25.00
Bowl, 9½", vegetable		85.00
Creamer	8.00	18.00
Cup	4.00	17.50
Mayonnaise, w/ladle	17.50	
Plate, 6", bread and butter	2.50	9.00
Plate, 8¼", luncheon	6.50	15.00
Plate, 9⅝", dinner	9.50	25.00
Plate, 11¼", sandwich	13.50	35.00
Saucer	1.50	5.00
Sugar	8.00	17.50

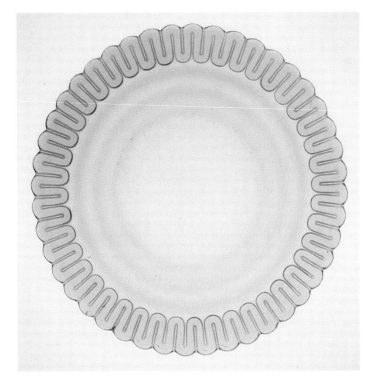

COIN GLASS #1372 FOSTORIA GLASS COMPANY, 1958-1982

Colors: amber, blue, crystal, green, olive green, and red.

Coin glass is rapidly becoming a hot collectible in today's markets. Coin glass is currently being made by Lancaster Colony who bought the Fostoria Company. The Coin pieces in production now do not have frosted coins! In fact, all prices below are for pieces that have frosted coins. I have heard it said that those pieces without frosted coins were sold only in the outlet stores. OK, that may be true; but I know that I saw the frosted coin pieces in the outlet stores back in the late 1970's and early 1980's when I first started working on my *Elegant Glassware of the Depression Era*. I was trying to keep up with the American pattern issues that were being made at that time, so I made many trips to outlet stores in Cambridge, Ohio, and Wheeling, West Virginia, during that time. By the way, unfrosted pieces can still be frosted today with the right equipment.

The blue color currently manufactured is a different shade of blue than that originally made; so if you see blue without frosted coins, beware!

The Olive Green is sometimes referred to as avocado, but Olive was the official name. The Green which is most desired is often called emerald by collectors. This color is represented by the jelly shown with the crystal on page 29.

You will find some crystal with gold decorated coins. This sells for about double the price of normal crystal if the gold is not worn.

	Amber	Blue	Crystal	Green	Olive	Ruby
Ash tray, 5" #1372/123	17.50	25.00	18.00	30.00	17.50	22.50
Ash tray, 7½", center coin #1372/119	20.00		25.00	35.00		25.00
Ash tray, 7½", round #1372/114	25.00	40.00	25.00	45.00	30.00	20.00
Ash tray, 10" #1372/124	30.00	50.00	25.00	55.00	30.00	
Ash tray, oblong #1372/115	15.00	20.00	10.00	25.00	25.00	
Ash tray/cover, 3" #1372/110	20.00	25.00	25.00	30.00		
Bowl, 8", round #1372/179	30.00	50.00	25.00	70.00	25.00	45.00
Bowl, 8½", ftd. #1372/199	60.00	85.00	50.00	100.00	50.00	70.00
Bowl, 8½", ftd. w/cover #1372/212	100.00	150.00	85.00	175.00		
Bowl, 9", oval #1372/189	30.00	55.00	30.00	70.00	30.00	50.00
*Bowl, wedding w/cover #1372/162	70.00	90.00	55.00	125.00	55.00	85.00
Candle holder, 4½", pr. #1372/316	30.00	50.00	40.00	50.00	30.00	50.00
Candle holder, 8", pr. #1372/326	60.00		50.00		50.00	95.00
Candy box w/cover, 4⅛" #1372/354	30.00	60.00	30.00	75.00	30.00	60.00
*Candy jar w/cover, 6⁵⁄₁₆" #1372/347	25.00	50.00	25.00	75.00	25.00	50.00
*Cigarette box w/cover, 5¾" x 4½" #1372/374	50.00	75.00	40.00	100.00		
Cigarette holder w/ash tray cover #1372/372	50.00	75.00	45.00	90.00		
Cigarette urn, 3⅜", ftd. #1372/381	25.00	45.00	20.00	50.00	20.00	40.00
Condiment set, 4 pc. (tray, 2 shakers and cruet) #1372/737	210.00	270.00	130.00		205.00	
Condiment tray, 9⅝", #1372/738	60.00	75.00	40.00		75.00	
Creamer #1372/680	11.00	16.00	10.00	30.00	15.00	16.00
Cruet, 7 oz. w/stopper #1372/531	65.00	100.00	50.00	150.00	80.00	
*Decanter w/stopper, pint, 10³⁄₁₆" #1372/400	120.00	160.00	80.00	325.00	120.00	
Jelly #1372/448	17.50	25.00	15.00	35.00	15.00	25.00
Lamp chimney, coach or patio #1372/461	45.00	60.00	35.00			
Lamp chimney, handled courting #1372/292	35.00	60.00				
Lamp, 9¾", handled courting, oil #1372/310	100.00	150.00				
Lamp, 10⅛", handled courting, electric #1372/311	100.00	150.00				
Lamp, 13½", coach, electric #1372/321	125.00	175.00	95.00			
Lamp, 13½", coach, oil #1372/320	125.00	175.00	95.00			
Lamp, 16⅝", patio, electric #1372/466	145.00	250.00	125.00			
Lamp, 16⅝", patio, oil #1372/459	145.00	250.00	125.00			
Nappy, 4½" #1372/495			18.00			
Nappy, 5⅜", w/hndl #1372/499	20.00	30.00	15.00	40.00	18.00	30.00
Pitcher, 32 oz., 6⁵⁄₁₆" #1372/453	50.00	100.00	45.00	125.00	50.00	80.00
Plate, 8", #1372/550			20.00		20.00	40.00

* Gold coins double price of crystal

Please refer to Foreword for pricing information

COIN GLASS #1372 (Cont.)

	Amber	Blue	Crystal	Green	Olive	Ruby
Punch bowl base #1372/602			150.00			
Punch bowl, 14", 1½" gal., #1372/600			150.00			
Punch cup #1372/615			30.00			
Salver, ftd., 6½" tall #1372/630	110.00	150.00	90.00	250.00	115.00	
Shaker, 3¼", pr. w/chrome top #1372/652	30.00	45.00	25.00	90.00	30.00	45.00
Stem, 4", 5 oz. wine #1372/26			30.00		45.00	60.00
Stem, 5¼", 9 oz., sherbet, #1372/7			20.00		40.00	60.00
Stem, 10½ oz., goblet #1372/2			30.00		45.00	85.00
Sugar w/cover #1372/673	35.00	45.00	25.00	60.00	30.00	45.00
Tumbler, 3⅝", 9 oz. juice/old fashioned #1372/81			27.50			
Tumbler, 4¼", 9 oz. water, scotch & soda #1372/73			27.50			
Tumbler, 5⅛", 12 oz. ice tea/high ball #1372/64			35.00			
Tumbler, 5⅜", 10 oz. double old fashioned #1372/23			20.00			
Tumbler, 5³⁄₁₆", 14 oz. ice tea #1372/58			30.00		40.00	75.00
Urn, 12¾", ftd., w/cover #1372/829	80.00	125.00	75.00	200.00	80.00	100.00
Vase, 8", bud #1372/799	22.00	40.00	20.00	60.00	25.00	45.00
Vase, 10", ftd. #1372/818			45.00			

"DAISY," NUMBER 620 INDIANA GLASS COMPANY

Colors: crystal, 1933-40; fired-on red, late 30's; amber, 1940's; dark green and milk glass, 1960's, 1970's, 1980's.

Daisy is a pattern that fits both 1930's and 1950's books; so a decision had to be made as to placement. Since more collectors search for the amber or green Daisy, I decided that it best fit this book instead of *The Collector's Encyclopedia of Depression Glass.* Know that the crystal was made in 1930's, but there are few collectors of that color. Fifteen patterns that are in this book are presently still in the other book, but next time Daisy will only be in this book.

Amber Daisy has always been one of the few amber colored glasswares that continued an upward pricing trend. Other amber glasswares have had ups and downs, but Daisy has always been steady. Add to that some difficult to find pieces, particularly the 12 oz. footed tea, 9⅜" berry and the cereal bowls, and you have a desirable collectible!

Avocado colored Daisy was marketed by Indiana as "Heritage" in the 1960's thru 1980's and not under the name Daisy or No. 620 as it was when it was first produced in the late 1930's. I mention this because Federal Glass Company also made a "Heritage" pattern that is rare in green. When I was in the hospital in 1983, I received a floral bouquet in a green Daisy 7⅜" berry bowl. It was embossed 1981 in the bottom!

The pattern shot below shows the indented grill plate, which holds the cream soup and not the cup. The bottom of the cream soup fits it exactly, while the cup bottom is too small for the ring.

There are a few pieces of red fired-on Daisy being found. A reader's letter last year said that her family had a red set that was purchased in 1935. So, that helps date this production. There is a pitcher in a fired-on red being found with this red and also the No. 618 tumblers. This pitcher does not belong to either pattern per se, but was sold with both of these Indiana patterns.

	Crystal	Green	Red, Amber		Crystal	Green	Red, Amber
Bowl, 4½", berry	4.00	5.00	8.00	Plate, 9⅜", dinner	5.00	6.00	8.00
Bowl, 4½", cream soup	4.00	5.00	10.00	Plate, 10⅜", grill w/indent			
Bowl, 6", cereal	9.00	11.00	25.00	for cream soup		12.50	
Bowl, 7⅜", deep berry	7.00	8.00	12.50	Plate, 11½", cake or sandwich	6.00	7.00	12.00
Bowl, 9⅜", deep berry	12.00	15.00	27.50	Platter, 10¾"	7.00	8.00	12.50
Bowl, 10", oval vegetable	9.00	10.00	15.00	Relish dish, 8⅜", 3 part	10.00		25.00
Creamer, footed	5.00	4.50	7.50	Saucer	1.00	1.00	1.50
Cup	3.50	3.50	5.50	Sherbet, footed	4.50	5.00	8.00
Plate, 6", sherbet	1.50	1.50	2.00	Sugar, footed	5.00	4.50	7.50
Plate, 7⅜", salad	3.00	3.00	6.50	Tumbler, 9 oz., footed	9.00	9.00	17.50
Plate, 8⅜", luncheon	3.50	4.00	5.00	Tumbler, 12 oz., footed	18.50	18.50	32.50

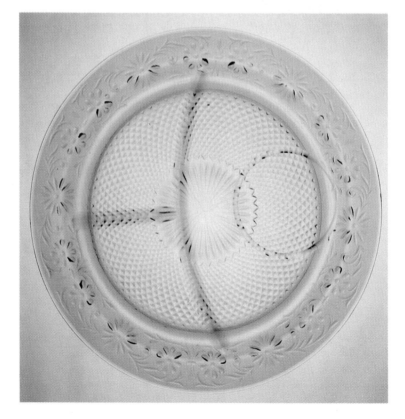

DEWDROP JEANNETTE GLASS COMPANY, 1953-1956

Color: crystal.

For several years I have been asked by collectors to consider putting Dewdrop in my *The Collector's Encyclopedia of Depression Glass*, but it was made in the mid 1950's; so it better fits the time period of this book.

The butter dish does have a bottom, but I could not find one to go with the top when I needed it for the photography session. You might think the butter bottom is hard to find by looking at my picture, but not so according to several people who have been collecting Dewdrop for years. I was told that the base to the punch bowl, candy dish and tumblers are the hardest pieces to find. I have actually owned very little of this pattern myself, but it sells very quickly when I do have it in stock.

	Crystal
Bowl, 4¾"	3.50
Bowl, 8½"	10.00
Bowl, 10⅜"	15.00
Butter, w/cover	25.00
Candy dish, w/cover, 7", round	17.50
Creamer	7.50
Cup, punch or snack	4.00
Pitcher, ½ gallon	22.50
Plate, 11½"	15.00
Plate, snack, w/indent for cup	4.50
Punch bowl base	8.50
Punch bowl, 6 qt.	22.50
Relish, leaf shape w/hndl.	7.50
Sugar, w/cover	12.50
Tray, 13", lazy susan	15.00
Tumbler, 9 oz., water	7.50
Tumbler, 15 oz., iced tea	10.00

33

EMERALD CREST FENTON ART GLASS COMPANY, 1949-1955

Color: white with green edge.

Emerald Crest was introduced in 1949 and was listed in Fenton catalogues until January, 1955. That means production was finished at least by the end of 1955. This popular line followed the Aqua Crest (blue trimmed) started in 1941; and Silver Crest (crystal trimmed) started in 1943. Silver Crest is included in this book beginning on page 130. Aqua crest will have to come at a later date, but prices fall between that of Emerald Crest and Silver Crest.

Some pieces of Emerald Crest have two different line numbers on them. Originally, this line was #680 and all pieces carried that designation. In July, 1952, Fenton began issuing a "Ware Number" for each piece. That is why you see two different numbers for the different sized plates.

Most mayonnaise sets are found with crystal spoons, but a green one was made. It is rarely found!

	White w/green
Basket, 5" #7236	65.00
Basket, 7" #7237	85.00
Bowl, 5", finger or deep dessert #7221	17.50
Bowl, 5½", soup #680, #7230	35.00
Bowl, 8½", flared #680	37.50
Bowl, 9½" #682	55.00
Bowl, 10" salad #7220	65.00
Bowl, dessert, shallow #7222	18.00
Bowl, ftd., tall, square #7330	65.00
Cake plate, 13" high ftd. #680, #7213	75.00
Cake plate, low ftd. #5813	65.00
Candle holder, flat saucer base, pr. #680	70.00
Comport, 6", ftd., flared #206	35.00
Comport, ftd., double crimped	35.00
Creamer, clear reeded hndls #7231	40.00
Cup #7208	32.50
Flower pot w/attached saucer #7299	65.00
Mayonnaise bowl, #7203	30.00
Mayonnaise ladle, crystal #7203	5.00
Mayonnaise ladle, green, #7203	30.00
Mayonnaise liner, #7203	10.00
Mayonnaise set, 3 pc. w/crys. ladle #7203	50.00
Mayonnaise set, 3 pc. w/gr. ladle #7203	70.00
Mustard, w/lid and spoon	75.00
Oil bottle, w/green stopper #680, #7269	80.00
Pitcher, 6" hndl., beaded melon #7116	50.00
Plate, 5½" #680, #7218	12.50
Plate, 6½" #680, #7219	15.00
Plate, 8½" #680, #7217	30.00
Plate, 10" #680, #7210	37.50
Plate, 12" #680, #7212	45.00
Plate, 12" #682	45.00
Plate, 16", torte #7216	60.00
Saucer #7208	12.50
Sherbet, ftd. #7226	20.00
Sugar, clear reeded hndls. #7231	35.00
Tid-bit, 2 tier plates #7297	55.00
Tid-bit, 3 tier plates #7298	75.00
Vase, 4½", fan #36, #7355	22.50
Vase, 6¼", fan #36, #7357	25.00
Vase, 8", bulbous base #186	50.00

FIRE-KING DINNERWARE "ALICE"
ANCHOR HOCKING GLASS CORPORATION, early 1940's

Colors: Jade-ite, white w/trims of blue or red.

"Alice" dinner plates are still elusive. No one has offered a better explanation than my assumption in my last book: "since the cup and saucers were packed in 'Mother's' oats and the dinners had to be purchased, it may be that no one was willing to buy dinner plates to go with the cup and saucers." If anyone else has a better explanation, let me know.

You will find "Alice" with white plates and with white trimmed in red or blue. Some of the red trimmed pieces fade to pink and there are two shades of blue trimmed pieces being found. I have seen more of the "Alice" with the blue or red trim in Texas than any place else. Of course, it sells best there also.

	Jade-ite	White/trim
Cup	2.50	7.50
Plate, 9½"	12.50	15.00
Saucer	1.00	2.50

FIRE-KING DINNERWARE CHARM
ANCHOR HOCKING GLASS CORPORATION, 1950-1954

Colors: Azur-ite, Jad-ite, Forest Green and Royal Ruby.

Charm refers to the square shaped dishes made by Anchor Hocking from 1950 through 1954. The Jad-ite and Azur-ite were advertised alongside the Forest Green and Royal Ruby; however, the color names of Forest Green and Royal Ruby prevailed on those squared shapes instead of Charm. Prices for those colors will be found under their respective names instead of under Charm.

The 8⅜" plate is listed in 1950 as a dinner plate, but later as a luncheon plate. Evidently, catalogue writers at Hocking felt that 8⅜" was a mighty small dinner plate and changed its designation after the first year.

For such a heavily promoted pattern, there is a shortage creamers, sugars and platters in both colors.

	Jad-ite	Azur-ite
Bowl, 4¾", dessert	4.00	6.50
Bowl, 7⅜", salad	7.50	12.50
Creamer	5.50	9.50
Cup	3.00	6.50
Plate, 6⅝", salad	3.00	4.00
Plate, 8⅜", luncheon	4.50	7.50
Platter, 11" x 8"	10.00	12.50
Saucer, 5⅜"	.75	1.50
Sugar	5.50	9.50

FIRE-KING DINNERWARE FLEURETTE and HONEYSUCKLE
ANCHOR HOCKING GLASS CORPORATION, 1958-1960

Color: white w/decal.

Fleurette first appears in Anchor Hocking's 1959-1960 catalogue printed in 4/58 and Honeysuckle the following year. Both patterns seems to have given way to Primrose by the 1960-1961 catalogue.

I might caution you that lead based paint was used on patterns during this time frame; so if you consider using them daily, proceed with caution. Remember the big clamor over some fast food chain's giveaway cartoon glasses in the early 1980's. These dishes used the same type process in their manufacture. I just wanted to warn you that if you eat off of them for 175 years, you will probably get wrinkles— or your IQ might slip a point.

I have enclosed catalogue sheets for Fleurette on pages 39-42 and Honeysuckle on page 43. Note on page 41 the various size sets of Fleurette that were available: 16 pc., 19 pc., 35 pc., and 53 pc. On page 42, you can see the actual selling prices of these sets.

There were three sizes of tumblers listed for the Honeysuckle set, but none were listed for Fleurette.

	Fleurette	Honeysuckle
Bowl, 4⅝", dessert	1.50	1.75
Bowl, 6⅝", soup plate	3.00	3.50
Bowl, 8¼", vegetable	5.00	5.50
Creamer	3.00	3.00
Cup, 8 oz.	3.00	3.50
Plate, 6¼", bread and butter	1.00	
Plate, 7⅜", salad	2.00	2.25
Plate, 9⅛", dinner	3.00	3.50
Platter, 9" x 12"	7.50	8.00
Saucer, 5¾"	.50	.50
Sugar	2.50	2.50
Sugar cover	2.00	2.00
Tumbler, 5 oz., juice		3.00
Tumbler, 9 oz., water		4.00
Tumbler, 12 oz., iced tea		5.00

Starter Set

16 pieces
HEAT
PROOF

Fleurette
DINNERWARE

FLEURETTE® DINNERWARE

W4679/58 — W4629/58

W4674/58

W4637/58 — W4638/58 — W4641/58

		PACKING	
W4679/58—8 oz. Cup		6 doz. — 25 lbs.	
W4629/58—5 ¾" Saucer		6 doz. — 27 lbs.	
W4674/58—4 ⅝" Dessert		6 doz. — 21 lbs.	
W4637/58—6 ¼" Bread & Butter Plate		3 doz. — 16 lbs.	
W4638/58—7 ⅜" Salad Plate		3 doz. — 23 lbs.	
W4641/58—9 ⅛" Dinner Plate		3 doz. — 39 lbs.	

W4667/58

Fleurette
Prepacked Sets
are shown on
Page 3.

W4647/58

W4667/58— 6 ⅝" Soup Plate		3 doz. — 27 lbs.	
W4647/58—12 x 9" Platter		1 doz. — 20 lbs.	

W4678/58

See Prepacked
Serva-Snack Set
on Page 3.

W4653/58 — W4654/58

W4678/58—8 ¼" Vegetable Bowl		1 doz. — 15 lbs.	
W4653/58— Sugar & Cover		2 doz. — 16 lbs.	
W4654/58— Creamer		2 doz. — 12 lbs.	

HEAT-PROOF

FLEURETTE® PREPACKED SETS

W4600/4—16 Pce. Starter Set
Each Set in Gift Display Carton,
4 Sets to Shipping Carton — 37 lbs.
COMPOSITION:
Four W4679/58 Cups
Four W4629/58 Saucers
Four W4674/58 Desserts
Four W4641/58 Dinner Plates

W4600/2—35 Pce. Dinner Set
Each Set in Shipping Carton — 21 lbs.
COMPOSITION:
Six W4679/58 Cups   One W4678/58 Vegetable Bowl
Six W4629/58 Saucers   One W4647/58 Platter
Six W4674/58 Desserts   One W4653/58 Sugar & Cover
Six W4638/58 Salad Plates   One W4654/58 Creamer
Six W4641/58 Dinner Plates

W4600/1—19 Pce. Luncheon Set (Not Illustrated)
Each Set in Gift Carton, 4 Sets to Shipping Carton — 41 lbs.
COMPOSITION:
Four W4679/58 Cups   Four W4641/58 Dinner Plates
Four W4629/58 Saucers   One W4653/58 Sugar & Cover
Four W4674/58 Desserts   One W4654/58 Creamer

W4600/3—53 Pce. Dinner Set (Not Illustrated)
Each Set in Shipping Carton — 32 lbs.
COMPOSITION:
Eight W4679/58 Cups   Eight W4641/58 Dinner Plates
Eight W4629/58 Saucers   One W4678/58 Vegetable Bowl
Eight W4674/58 Desserts   One W4647/58 Platter
Eight W4638/58 Salad Plates One W4653/58 Sugar & Cover
Eight W4667/58 Soup Plates   One W4654/58 Creamer

SERVA-SNACK SET

W4600/9—8 Pce. Snack Set
Each Set in Die-Cut Display Carton,
6 Sets to Shipping Carton — 48 lbs.

COMPOSITION:
Four 5 oz. Cups
Four 11 x 6" Rectangular Trays

(See Crystal Serva-Snack Sets on Page 10.)

PROMOTE PREPACKED SETS

HEAT-PROOF

Fleurette

W4674/58

W4678/58

HEAT-PROOF

W4647/58

W4667/58

W4653/58

W4679/58 — W4629/58

W4654/58

OPEN STOCK		Per Doz. Net Pkd.	Doz. Ctn.	Wt. Ctn.
W4679/58—	8 oz. Cup	$ .90	6	25#
W4629/58—	5¾" Saucer	.90	6	28#
W4674/58—	4⅝" Dessert	.90	6	21#
W4637/58—	6¼" B & B Plate	1.20	3	16#
W4638/58—	7⅜" Salad Plate	1.50	3	23#
W4667/58—	6⅝" Soup Plate	1.60	3	24#
W4641/58—	9⅛" Dinner Plate	1.80	3	39#
W4678/58—	8¼" Vegetable Bowl	2.40	1	14#
W4647/58—	12 x 9" Platter	3.60	1	20#
W4653/58—	Sugar & Cover	1.50	2	11#
W4654/58—	Creamer	1.25	2	12#

SETS

W4600/4—16 PCE. STARTER SET .... **$1.55 Set** 4 Sets 39#
(Each Set in Gift Display Ctn.)
COMPOSITION: Four each Cups, Saucers,
Desserts and Dinner Plates

W4600/1—19 PCE. LUNCHEON SET .. **1.75 Set** 4 Sets 40#
(Each Set in Gift Carton)
COMPOSITION: Four each Cups, Saucers,
Desserts and Dinner Plates.
One Sugar & Cover and one Creamer.

W4600/2—35 PCE. DINNER SET .... **3.95 Set** 1 Set 21#
(Each Set in Shipping Carton)
COMPOSITION: Six each Cups, Saucers,
Desserts, Salad Plates and Dinner Plates.
One each Vegetable Bowl, Platter,
Sugar & Cover and Creamer.

W4600/3—53 PCE. DINNER SET .... **6.00 Set** 1 Set 32#
(Each Set in Shipping Carton)
COMPOSITION: Eight each Cups, Saucers,
Desserts, Salad Plates, Soup Plates and
Dinner Plates. One each Vegetable Bowl,
Platter, Sugar & Cover and Creamer.

Anchorglass ®

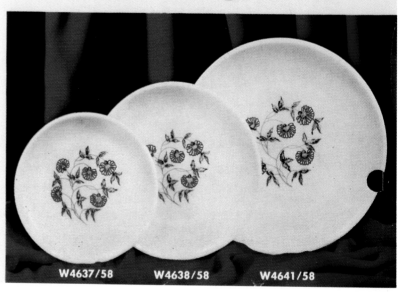

W4637/58   W4638/58   W4641/58

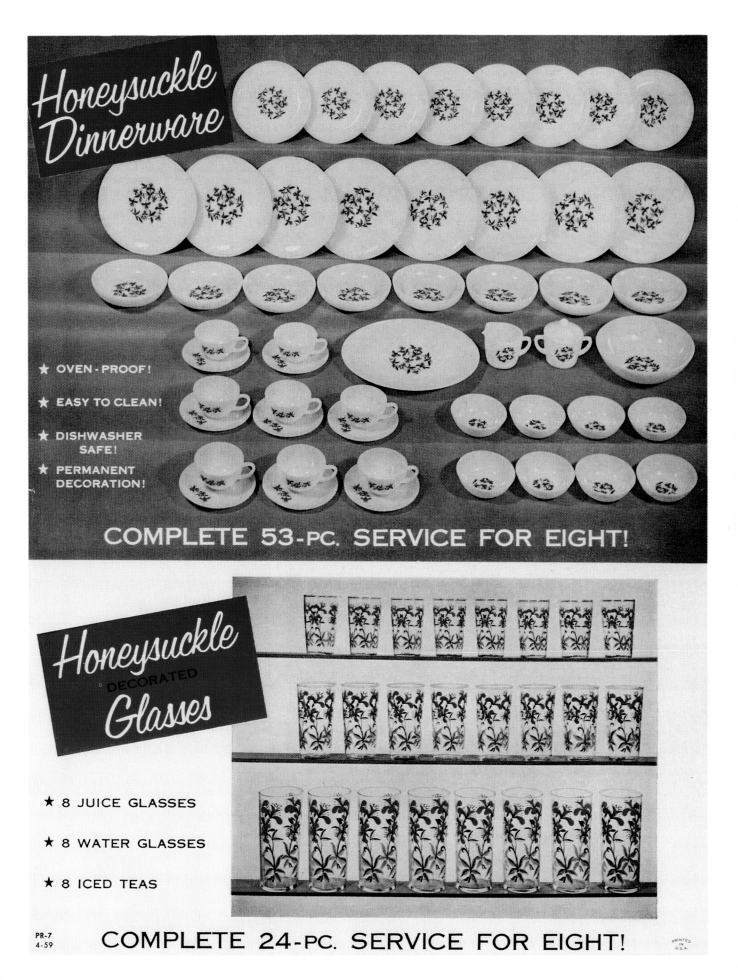

Honeysuckle
Dinnerware

★ OVEN - PROOF!

★ EASY TO CLEAN!

★ DISHWASHER SAFE!

★ PERMANENT DECORATION!

COMPLETE 53-PC. SERVICE FOR EIGHT!

Honeysuckle
DECORATED
Glasses

★ 8 JUICE GLASSES

★ 8 WATER GLASSES

★ 8 ICED TEAS

PR-7
4-59

COMPLETE 24-PC. SERVICE FOR EIGHT!

PRINTED IN U.S.A.

43

FIRE-KING DINNERWARE "GAME BIRD"
ANCHOR HOCKING GLASS CORPORATION, 1959-1962

Color: white w/decal decoration.

    Anchor Hocking called these both "Wild Bird" and Game Bird," but the "Game Bird" seems more apropos. I have catalogue sheets of mugs, cereals and ash trays listed for 1960-1961; but as you can see below, there are many more pieces available than those.

    You will find the following birds on this pattern: "Canada Goose," Ringed-Necked Pheasant," "Ruffled Grouse" and "Mallard Duck."

    Finding each bird on each piece may be a problem. The only sugar and creamer I have seen are decorated with Ringed-Necked Pheasants; I do not know if you can find other birds on these pieces or not. It may be possible to collect a whole set of Pheasant decorated dinnerware and nothing else can be collected in a full set. As I do not have complete catalogue information available, that is only a guess until one of you readers can send me information otherwise.

    There is quite an interest in collecting this macho set among the males who used to be dragged to Depression Glass shows so they could pay for the purchases and tote them to the car. Now, there are many of these former toters only who are also spenders.

	White w/decals
Ash tray, 5¼"	5.00
Bowl, 4⅝", dessert	3.75
Bowl, 5", soup or cereal	5.50
Bowl, 8¼", vegetable	10.00
Creamer	6.00
Mug, 8 oz.	7.50
Plate, 7⅜", salad	3.00
Plate, 9⅛", dinner	5.00
Sugar	5.00
Sugar cover	2.00
Tumbler, 11 oz., iced tea	6.00

Anchorwhite heat-resistant Mugs and Bowls

With authentic game bird decorations

Colorful game bird decorations lend a touch of rustic charm to these practical Anchorwhite mugs and bowls. The mugs are as ideal for in-home use as they are for outdoors. Versatile, too, they're perfect for coffee as well as for cocoa, hot chocolate and milk. The cereal-soup bowls, with their matching decorations, will brighten up any table setting. Both mugs and bowls are heat-resistant and safe to use with hot liquids and foods.

No.	Size	Item	Doz. Ctn.	Lbs. Ctn.
W1212/5931	8 oz.	Ruffed Grouse Mug	4	27
W1212/5932	8 oz.	Ring-Necked Pheasant Mug	4	27
W1212/5933	8 oz.	Canada Goose Mug	4	27
W1212/5934	8 oz.	Mallard Duck Mug	4	27
W291/5931	5″	Ruffed Grouse Bowl	4	27
W291/5932	5″	Ring-Necked Pheasant Bowl	4	27
W291/5933	5″	Canada Goose Bowl	4	27
W291/5934	5″	Mallard Duck Bowl	4	27

ANCHOR HOCKING GLASS CORPORATION
Lancaster, Ohio, U.S.A.

FIRE-KING DINNERWARE JADE-ITE "JANE RAY"
ANCHOR HOCKING GLASS CORPORATION, 1945-1963

"Jane Ray" is one of the most collected of the Anchor Hocking patterns. A Jade-ite set is possible to attain in this color and many collectors are using the restaurant ware line to supplement "Jane Ray." Demitasse sets are the most difficult pieces to find with collectors shelling out a twenty dollar bill to purchase them. Platters and soup bowls are also scarce for this normally easy to find pattern.

A 1947 chain store listing of glassware by Anchor Hocking lists this as "Jade-ite Heat Proof Tableware." This listing also records the vegetable bowl as 8⅛" instead of 8¼" as listed in later catalogues.

Availability, just as blue Bubble was years ago, puts this pattern in front of many new collectors. Prices are rising due to the ever increasing demand of collectors for "Jane Ray."

	Jade-ite
Bowl, 4⅞", dessert	3.00
Bowl, 5⅞", oatmeal	4.00
Bowl, 7⅝", soup plate	6.00
Bowl, 8¼", vegetable	8.00
Cup	2.00
Cup, demitasse	12.50
Creamer	4.00
Plate, 7¾", salad	3.50
Plate, 9⅛", dinner	5.00
Platter, 9" x 12"	10.50
Saucer	.75
Saucer, demitasse	7.50
Sugar	4.00
Sugar cover	4.00

FIRE-KING DINNERWARE JADE-ITE RESTAURANT WARE
ANCHOR HOCKING GLASS CORPORATION, 1950-1953

Collectors are becoming more aware of the Restaurant Ware line of Anchor Hocking because of its adaptability to microwave use. As far as I know, any of these pieces can be used this way. Remember to put the dish in the microwave for just a little time to see if it gets hot just as you would test any other dish. "Jane Ray" collectors started the rush on this Jade-ite and now there is not enough of this short-lived pattern to go around.

You can see a catalogue sheet on page 48 to show you the differences in the cups. The 5-compartment plate and the oval partitioned plates were already discontinued by 1953. They are in shorter supply than many other pieces; but then, not every collector wants these pieces.

	Jade-ite		Jade-ite
Bowl, 4¾", fruit G294	3.00	Plate, 8⅞", oval partitioned G211	7.50
Bowl, 8 oz., flanged rim, cereal G305	4.00	Plate, 8", luncheon G316	3.50
Bowl, 10 oz., deep G309	5.00	Plate, 9⅝", 3-compartment G292	3.50
Bowl, 15 oz., deep G300	7.50	Plate, 9¾", oval, sandwich G216	5.00
Cup, 6 oz., straight G215	4.00	Plate, 9⅝", 5-compartment G311	12.50
Cup, 7 oz., extra heavy G299	5.00	Plate, 9", dinner G306	5.00
Cup, 7 oz., narrow rim G319	5.00	Platter, 9½", oval G307	8.50
Mug, coffee, 7 oz. G212	5.00	Platter, 11½", oval G308	7.50
Plate, 5½", bread/butter G315	1.50	Saucer, 6" G295	1.25
Plate, 6¾", pie or salad G297	2.50		

Please refer to Foreword for pricing information

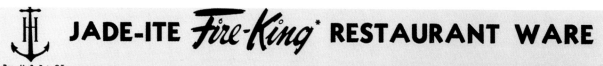

JADE-ITE *Fire-King** RESTAURANT WARE

Reg. U. S. Pat. Off. **INEXPENSIVE** ● **HEAT-RESISTANT** ● **RUGGED** ● **STAIN-RESISTANT** ● **SANITARY** ● **COLORFUL**

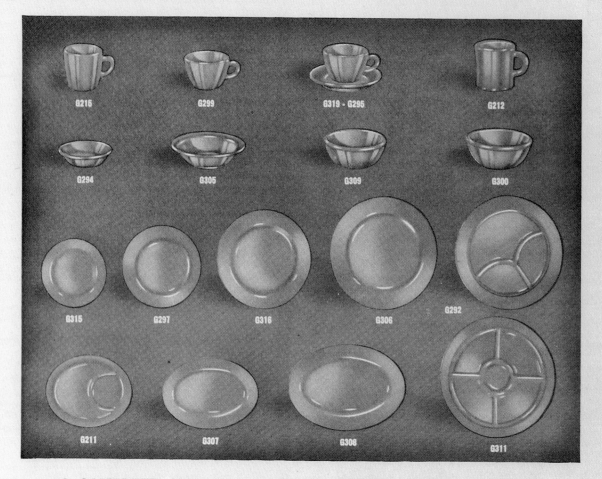

A COMPLETE SERVICE FOR MASS FEEDING ESTABLISHMENTS

Cat. No.	Description	Actual Size or Capacity	Std. Pkg.	Weight
G215	Cup (Straight)	6 oz.	4 doz.	35#
G299	Cup (Extra Heavy)	7 oz.	4 doz.	36#
G319	Cup (Narrow Rim)	7 oz.	4 doz.	32#
G295	Saucer	6″	4 doz.	31#
G212	Coffee Mug (Extra Heavy)	7 oz.	4 doz.	48#
G294	Fruit	4¾″	6 doz.	30#
G305	Grapefruit—Cereal	8 oz.	4 doz.	37#
G309	Bowl	10 oz.	4 doz.	30#
G300	Bowl	15 oz.	4 doz.	43#
G315	B & B Plate	5½″	4 doz.	30#
G297	Pie or Salad Plate	6¾″	4 doz.	35#
G316	Luncheon Plate	8″	2 doz.	26#
G306	Dinner Plate	9″	2 doz.	31#
G292	3-Compartment Plate	9⅝″	2 doz.	38#
G211	Oval Partitioned Plate	8⅞″	2 doz.	23#
G307	Oval Platter	9½″	2 doz.	24#
G308	Oval Platter	11½″	1 doz.	20#
G311	5-Compartment Plate	9⅝″	2 doz.	37#

*REG. U. S. PAT. OFF.

PRINTED IN U.S.A.

ANCHOR HOCKING GLASS CORP.
LANCASTER, OHIO, U. S. A.

FIRE-KING DINNERWARE PEACH LUSTRE/GRAY LAUREL
ANCHOR HOCKING GLASS CORPORATION, 1952-1963

Peach Lustre was introduced in 1952. The catalogue describes it as "The New Sensation." This name referred to the "laurel leaf" design which was also made into Gray Laurel in 1953 and only shown in gray in the 1953 catalogue. Peach Lustre continued until the 1963 catalogue; but during this time, the name was used for the **color** and not just the pattern. Page 50 is taken from a 1954 catalogue. The 11" serving plate was discontinued as of 8-25-60.

Gray Laurel is in far shorter supply than Peach Lustre since it only appeared in one Anchor Hocking catalogue. I found a set in Phoenix last year and have seen very little since then. Gray Laurel had three size tumblers that were made to go with it. These are "complementary decorated" in gray and maroon bands with 5 ounce juice, 9 ounce water and 13 ounce iced tea available.

Catalogue numbers are the same for each pattern with Gray Laurel having a "K" prefix and Peach Lustre using a "L" prefix.

The crystal stemware shown under Bubble and "Boopie" were also engraved with a "Laurel" cutting to go with these patterns.

	Gray Laurel	Peach Lustre		Gray Laurel	Peach Lustre
Bowl, 4⅞", dessert	3.00	2.50	Plate, 7⅜", salad	3.00	2.00
Bowl, 7⅝", soup plate	3.50	3.00	Plate, 9⅛", dinner	5.00	2.50
Bowl, 8¼", vegetable	6.50	6.00	Plate, 11", serving	9.50	7.50
Creamer, ftd.	3.00	2.50	Saucer, 5¾"	.50	.50
Cup, 8 oz.	3.50	3.00	Sugar, ftd.	3.00	2.50

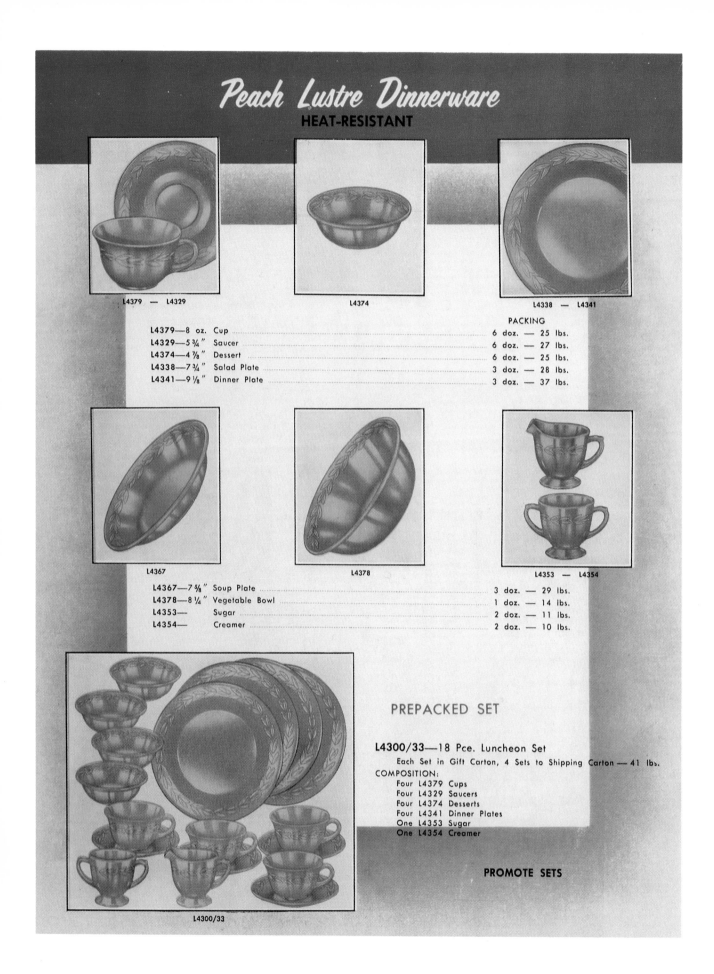

Peach Lustre Dinnerware
HEAT-RESISTANT

L4379 — L4329

L4374

L4338 — L4341

		PACKING
L4379—8 oz. Cup		6 doz. — 25 lbs.
L4329—5 ¾" Saucer		6 doz. — 27 lbs.
L4374—4 ⅞" Dessert		6 doz. — 25 lbs.
L4338—7 ¾" Salad Plate		3 doz. — 28 lbs.
L4341—9 ⅛" Dinner Plate		3 doz. — 37 lbs.

L4367

L4378

L4353 — L4354

L4367—7 ⅝" Soup Plate		3 doz. — 29 lbs.
L4378—8 ¼" Vegetable Bowl		1 doz. — 14 lbs.
L4353— Sugar		2 doz. — 11 lbs.
L4354— Creamer		2 doz. — 10 lbs.

L4300/33

PREPACKED SET

L4300/33—18 Pce. Luncheon Set

Each Set in Gift Carton, 4 Sets to Shipping Carton — 41 lbs.

COMPOSITION:
Four L4379 Cups
Four L4329 Saucers
Four L4374 Desserts
Four L4341 Dinner Plates
One L4353 Sugar
One L4354 Creamer

PROMOTE SETS

FIRE-KING DINNERWARE & OVENWARE PRIMROSE,
ANCHOR HOCKING GLASS CORPORATION, 1960-1962

Primrose was a pattern that Anchor Hocking used to bridge the gap between dinnerware and ovenware. Primrose was made for both uses with pieces designed for both jobs. Although many of Anchor Hocking's lines were issued as dinnerware, they are marked ovenware on the bottom to let customers know that they were "heat-proof" and could be "pre warmed" in the oven.

This seemed to be the pattern that was pushed in place of Fleurette and Honeysuckle, but Primrose may not have been as successful as many of Anchor Hocking's earlier Fire-King patterns since it was only listed in the 1960-1961 and 1961-1962 catalogues. From the present availability of the ovenware line, I suspect that it might be really scarce or many people from the 1960's are still using it!

All casserole covers are clear crystal Fire-King. All pieces of ovenware were guaranteed against oven breakage for two years. Dealers would exchange a new item for the broken pieces. The one quart casserole, baking pan and oval casserole were all sold with a brass finished candlewarmer and candle.

The deep loaf pan was sold as a baking pan by adding a glass cover.

	White w/decal		White w/decal		White w/decal
Bowl, 4⅝", dessert	1.75	Casserole, 2 qt., knob cover	10.00	Plate, 7⅜", salad	2.25
Bowl, 6⅝", soup plate	3.50	Creamer	3.00	Plate, 9⅛", dinner	3.50
Bowl, 8¼", vegetable	5.50	Cup, 5 oz., snack	2.50	Platter, 9" x 12"	8.00
Cake pan, 8", round	7.50	Cup, 8 oz.	3.00	Saucer, 5¾"	.50
Cake pan, 8", square	7.50	Custard, 6 oz., low or dessert	2.00	Sugar	2.50
Casserole, pt., knob cover	4.50	Pan, 5" x 9", baking, w/cover	10.00	Sugar cover	2.00
Casserole, ½ qt., oval,		Pan, 5" x 9", deep loaf	7.50	Tray, 11" x 6", rectangular, snack	3.00
au gratin cover	12.00	Pan, 6½" x 10½", utility baking	8.00	Tumbler, 5 oz., juice	3.00
Casserole, 1 qt., knob cover	7.00	Pan, 8" x 12½", utility baking	10.00	Tumbler, 9 oz., water	4.00
Casserole, 1½ qt., knob cover	8.50	Plate, 6¼", bread and butter	1.00	Tumbler, 13 oz., iced tea	5.00

NEW!
Primrose
Anchorwhite heat-resistant ovenware

The delicate red, tan and grey tones of stylized flowers enhance this new gleaming white ovenware. It's glamorous...on the table...in the kitchen. It's perfect for special occasions or everyday use ...just right for oven-to-table service, storing and reheating. Build more colorful displays with this eye-catching, traffic-stopping, Primrose Ovenware. It will sell on sight! Available in 8 and 11 piece sets in gift cartons...also in open stock.

ANCHOR HOCKING GLASS CORPORATION
Lancaster, Ohio, U. S. A.

W424/62

W410/62

W411/62

W450/62

W409/62

W452/62

New
Primrose
Anchorglass
Ovenware

Number	Size	Item	Doz. Ctn.	Lbs. Ctn.
W424/62	6 Oz.	Dessert	4	15
W405/62	1 Pt.	Casserole, Cover	1	16
W406/62	1 Qt.	Casserole, Cover	½	14
W407/62	1½ Qt.	Casserole, Cover	½	19
W467/62	1½ Qt.	Oval Casserole, Au Gratin Cover	½	19
W408/62	2 Qt.	Casserole, Cover	½	21
W450/62	8″	Round Cake Pan	½	12
W452/62	8″	Square Cake Pan	½	17
W409/62	5″ x 9″	Deep Loaf Pan	½	11
W410/62	6½″ x 10½″	Utility Baking Pan	½	15
W411/62	8″ x 12½″	Utility Baking Pan	½	23
W469/62	5″ x 9″	Baking Pan and Cover	½	21
W400/245*		8 Pc. Set	4 Sets	34
W400/246**		11 Pc. Set	4 Sets	53

*Composition: One each 1 qt. Casserole, Cover, 10½″ Utility Baking Pan, 8″ Round
Cake Pan; four 6 oz. Desserts, Gift Ctn.

**Composition: One each 1½ qt. Casserole, Cover, 5″ x 9″ Deep Loaf Pan, 8″ x 12½″
Utility Baking Pan, 8″ Square Cake Pan; six 6 oz. Desserts, Gift Ctn.

FIRE-KING OVEN GLASS ANCHOR HOCKING GLASS CORPORATION, 1942-1950's

Colors: Sapphire blue, crystal; some Ivory and Jade-ite.

Fire-King is one of the more easily recognized patterns in this book! Almost everyone remembers Grandma's cooking bread pudding (my Mom still uses her roaster bottom for that) or baking a pie (Cathy's grandmother did that) in Fire-King. Many pieces were handed down from mother to daughter and it is amazing how many Fire-King pieces are still being used! Fire-King had a two year guarantee to back up the durability of this oven proof glassware.

The skillet and nipple cover are shown compliments of Anchor-Hocking's photographer. The skillets are still in hiding, but several nipple covers have surfaced. Those blue covers are embossed "BINKY'S NIP CAP U.S.A." (and not Fire-King). The boxed set on page 56 has a Fire-King measuring cup, nipple cover, measuring spoons and nipples. The side of the box reads "Binky Formula Feeding Set, Glass Measuring Cup, Glass Nipple Protector, Plastic Funnel, Plastic Scoop, 4 Plastic Measuring Spoons, Binky Baby Products Co., NY., U.S.A." The brochure enclosed in the box states "BINKYTOYS - The Best for Baby for over a Quarter Century. BINKYTOYS meet every advocated requirement essential to baby's SAFETY - HEALTH - and WELL BEING."

Be careful using this in the microwave. It is fine for normal ovens, but it tends to develop heat cracks from sudden temperature changes when used in the microwave. (I know that from sad experience).

The dry cup measure has ounce measurements up the side and no spout for pouring.

One of the major problems with those juice saver pie plates is the heavy usage that most received. Many are heavily scratched. To obtain the price below, this pie plate has to be mint!

The prices with asterisks under Ivory are for Jade-ite items with the Fire-King **embossing**. All of the Ivory is plain with no design. You will find plain Ivory and Jade-ite mugs, but they hold 8 oz. and not seven. The Jade-ite mug with the embossed pattern is rare!

All listings below are from Anchor Hocking's Catalogue "L" with some additional catalogue items shown on page 57.

There are two styles of table servers being found; and you can find a casserole lid atop a Bersted Mfg. Co. popcorn popper. One of these can be seen in the fourth edition of my *Kitchen Glassware of the Depression Era*.

	Ivory	Sapphire		Ivory	Sapphire
Baker, 1 pt., 4½" x 5"		5.00	Loaf pan, 9⅛" x 5⅛", deep	12.50	17.50
Baker, 1 pt., round	3.00	4.50	Mug, coffee, 7 oz., 2 styles	*25.00	21.50
Baker, 1 qt., round	4.50	6.00	Nipple cover		125.00
Baker, 1½ qt., round	5.50	11.00	Nurser, 4 oz.		13.00
Baker, 2 qt., round	8.00	12.50	Nurser, 8 oz.		22.50
Baker, 6 oz., individual	2.50	3.50	Percolator top, 2⅛"		4.50
Bowl, 4⅜", individual pie plate		11.00	Pie plate, 8⅜", 1½" deep		7.00
Bowl, 5⅜", cereal or deep dish pie plate	6.00	12.00	Pie plate, 9⅝", 1½" deep		9.00
Bowl, measuring, 16 oz.		22.50	Pie plate, 9", 1½" deep	6.50	8.00
Cake pan (deep), 8¾" (½ roaster)		20.00	Pie plate, 10⅜", juice saver	*50.00	65.00
Cake pan, 9"	12.50		Refrigerator jar & cover, 4½" x 5"	**7.50	10.00
Casserole, 1 pt., knob handle cover	8.00	11.00	Refrigerator jar & cover, 5⅛" x 9⅛"	**15.00	30.00
Casserole, 1 qt., knob handle cover	9.50	12.00	Roaster, 8¾"		40.00
Casserole, 1 qt., pie plate cover		16.00	Roaster, 10⅜"		60.00
Casserole, 1½ qt., knob handle cover	11.00	12.50	Table server, tab handles (hot plate)	8.50	15.00
Casserole, 1½ qt., pie plate cover		16.00	Utility bowl, 6⅞", 1 qt.		10.00
Casserole, 2 qt., knob handle cover	13.00	18.00	Utility bowl, 8⅜", 1½ qt.		14.00
Casserole, 2 qt., pie plate cover		20.00	Utility bowl, 10⅛"		15.00
Casserole, individual, 10 oz.		12.50	Utility pan, 8⅛" x 12½", 2 qt.		30.00
Cup, 8 oz. measuring, 1 spout		16.00	Utility pan, 10½" x 2" deep	12.00	20.00
Cup, 8 oz., dry measure, no spout		150.00			
Cup, 8 oz., measuring, 3 spout		18.00	*Jade-ite w/embossed design		
Custard cup or baker, 5 oz.	2.50	3.00	**Jade-ite		
Custard cup or baker, 6 oz.	3.00	3.50			

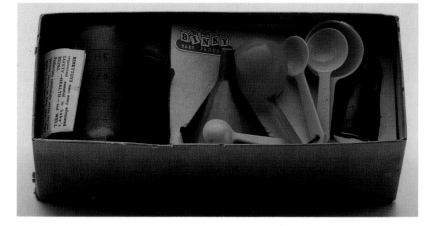

FIRE - KING OVEN GLASS

Housewives prefer to cook in glass for they are then able to actually see their foods cooking, eliminating the possibility of improperly cooked foods. Glass is also more easily cleaned than metal utensils, saving time and labor.

A three-fold purpose—bake, serve, and store in the same dish. Fire-King oven glass is not only suitable for oven cooking but makes ideal serving dishes for the table and in addition is safe and practical for refrigerator use.

Not only does Fire-King possess unusual cooking qualities but it is attractive, a complement to any table, and above all—the lowest priced oven glass on the market.

57

FIRE-KING OVEN WARE, TURQUOISE BLUE ANCHOR HOCKING GLASS
CORPORATION, 1957-1958

Color: Turquoise Blue.

Although Turquoise Blue was advertised as dinnerware, all pieces are marked ovenware as is the case of most of Anchor Hocking's dinnerware. Turquoise Blue has gotten so popular that a couple of dealers who laughed at our $17.50 price on 10" plates a couple of years ago are now collecting this pattern and recently asked if we had any of them left. We didn't! When you search for and use a pattern for five years as we did this one, several observations about buying or using it come to mind. The 10" plates are rare and not available in any quantity. As far as I am concerned, it is an ideal size dinner plate. (The normal 9" dinner with its upturned edges does not hold enough for my boys.) Soup and cereal bowls are not commonly found and are probably underpriced in today's market.

The batter bowl was never shown in catalogues and the 5¾" ash tray was discontinued before the 1957-58 catalogue was out of print. The three part relish, egg plate and the snack sets were heavily promoted with 22K gold decorations. Do not put the gold edged pieces in the microwave since the gold causes sparks. All other pieces worked well in our microwave.

Cups, saucers, creamer and sugar are easily found. The 9" dinner plates and mugs are the next easiest pieces to accumulate. The 6⅛" and 7" plates are not quite as hard to find as the 10" plates, but they are both scarce. Numerous collectors of this pattern have told me they have never seen either one! Although the 9" plate with cup indent is not as plentiful as the dinner plate, it does not command the price of the dinner since not everyone wants to own these snack sets... yet!

	Blue		Blue
Ash tray, 3½"	6.00	Bowl, round, mixing, 3 qt.	10.00
Ash tray, 4⅝"	8.00	Bowl, round, mixing, 4 qt.	12.50
Ash tray, 5¾"	12.50	Creamer	5.00
Batter bowl, w/spout	42.50	Cup	4.00
Bowl, 4½", berry	5.00	Egg plate, 9¾"	12.50
Bowl, 5", cereal	8.00	Mug, 8 oz.	8.00
Bowl, 6⅝", soup/salad	12.00	Plate, 6⅛"	8.00
Bowl, 8", vegetable	12.50	Plate, 7"	9.00
Bowl, tear, mixing, 1 pt.	9.00	Plate, 9"	6.50
Bowl, tear, mixing, 1 qt.	12.00	Plate, 9", w/cup indent	6.00
Bowl, tear, mixing, 2 qt.	15.00	Plate, 10"	22.50
Bowl, tear, mixing, 3 qt.	18.00	Relish, 3 part, 11⅛"	10.00
Bowl, round, mixing, 1 qt.	10.00	Saucer	1.00
Bowl, round, mixing, 2 qt.	8.00	Sugar	5.00

TURQUOISE-BLUE TABLEWARE — HEAT-PROOF

B4079 — B4029

B4074

B4037 — B4038 — B4041 — B4046

PACKING

B4079—	8 oz.	Cup	6 doz. — 24 lbs.
B4029—	5 3/4"	Saucer	6 doz. — 32 lbs.
B4074—	4 5/8"	Dessert	6 doz. — 23 lbs.
B4037—	6 1/4"	Bread & Butter Plate	3 doz. — 18 lbs.
B4038—	7 1/4"	Salad Plate	3 doz. — 23 lbs.
B4041—	9"	Dinner Plate	3 doz. — 42 lbs.
B4046—	10"	Serving Plate	1 doz. — 18 lbs.

See Mixing Bowls on Page 27, Mug and Bowl on Page 23 and Ash Trays on Page 41.

B4067

B4078

B4053 — B4054

B4067—	6 5/8"	Soup Plate	3 doz. — 26 lbs.
B4078—	8 1/4"	Vegetable Bowl	1 doz. — 17 lbs.
B4053—		Sugar	2 doz. — 11 lbs.
B4054—		Creamer	2 doz. — 11 lbs.

B4000/18

PREPACKED SETS

B4000/18—12 Pce. Starter Set
Each Set in Display Style Carton, 6 Sets to Shipper — 48 lbs.
COMPOSITION: Four Each B4079 Cups, B4029 Saucers and B4041 Dinner Plates

B4000/19—18 Pce. Luncheon Set
Each Set in Gift Carton, 4 Sets to Shipper — 40 lbs.
COMPOSITION: Four Each B4079 Cups, B4029 Saucers, B4074 Desserts, and B4041 Dinner Plates; One Each B4053 Sugar and B4054 Creamer

B4000/21—34 Pce. Dinner Set
Each Set in Shipping Carton — 20 lbs.
COMPOSITION: Six Each B4079 Cups, B4029 Saucers, B4074 Desserts, B4038 Salad Plates and B4041 Dinner Plates; One Each B4078 Vegetable Bowl, B4046 Serving Plate, B4053 Sugar and B4054 Creamer

B4000/22—52 Pce. Dinner Set
Each Set in Shipping Carton — 32 lbs.
COMPOSITION: Eight Each B4079 Cups, B4029 Saucers, B4074 Desserts, B4038 Salad Plates, B4067 Soup Plates and B4041 Dinner Plates; One Each B4078 Vegetable Bowl, B4046 Serving Plate, B4053 Sugar and B4054 Creamer

FIRE-KING OVEN WARE, "SWIRL" ANCHOR HOCKING GLASS CORPORATION, 1950's

Colors: Azur-ite, Ivory, Ivory trimmed in gold or red, white or white trimmed in gold, and Pink.

I looked at the many "swirled" patterns that Anchor Hocking made starting with 1950 and spent a whole day trying to find a way to organize them into some sequence of order that made a little sense. First of all, **colors** determined name and not pattern which has been a major problem with Anchor Hocking. There were also two distinct swirled patterns and even a change in sugar styles. Finally, I came up with the following for this book. Swirls of the 1950's and Swirls of the 1960's...

The first "Swirl" was Azur-ite which is the light blue that is shown on page 65 followed by Sunrise (red trimmed, also shown on page 65) shortly thereafter. That was followed by Ivory White which was introduced in 1953 but in the mid 1950's this became Anchorwhite. If you find a flat white sugar or creamer, it is Ivory White; but finding a footed creamer or sugar means it is Anchorwhite. Golden Anniversary was introduced in 1955 by adding 22K gold trim to Ivory White and Pink was introduced in 1956.

	ANCHORWHITE IVORY WHITE	GOLDEN ANNIVERSARY	AZUR-ITE/PINK/ SUNRISE
Bowl, 4⅞", fruit or dessert	2.25	2.50	3.75
Bowl, 7¼", vegetable			7.50
Bowl, 7⅝", soup plate	2.50	2.75	4.50
Bowl, 8¼", vegetable	4.50	4.75	8.50
Creamer, flat	3.00		6.50
Creamer, ftd.	2.50	3.00	
Cup, 8 oz.	2.50	2.75	4.25
Plate, 7⅜", salad	2.00	2.25	3.50
Plate, 9⅛", dinner	2.75	3.25	6.00
Plate, 11", serving			10.00
Platter, 12" x 9"	5.50	6.00	12.50
Saucer, 5¾"	.50	.50	1.00
Sugar lid, for flat sugar	2.00		4.50
Sugar lid, for ftd. sugar	2.00		
Sugar, flat, tab handles	3.00		5.50
Sugar, ftd., open handles	2.50	3.00	
Tumbler, 5 oz., juice			4.00
Tumbler, 9 oz., water			5.00
Tumbler, 12 oz., iced tea			6.00

Please refer to Foreword for pricing information

GOLDEN ANNIVERSARY DINNERWARE

W4100/57

W4100/57—18 Pce. Luncheon Set

Each Set in Gift Carton, 4 Sets to Shipping Carton — 41 lbs.
COMPOSITION:

Four W4179/50 Cups	Four W4141/50 Dinner Plates
Four W4129/50 Saucers	One W4153/50 Sugar
Four W4174/50 Desserts	One W4154/50 Creamer

W4100/58—34 Pce. Dinner Set (Not illustrated)

Each Set in Shipping Carton — 23 lbs.
COMPOSITION:

Six W4179/50 Cups	One W4178/50 Vegetable Bowl
Six W4129/50 Saucers	One W4147/50 Platter
Six W4174/50 Desserts	One W4153/50 Sugar
Six W4138/50 Salad Plates	One W4154/50 Creamer
Six W4141/50 Dinner Plates	

W4100/59—52 Pce. Dinner Set (Not illustrated)

Each Set in Shipping Carton — 35 lbs.
COMPOSITION:

Eight W4179/50 Cups	Eight W4141/50 Dinner Plates
Eight W4129/50 Saucers	One W4178/50 Vegetable Bowl
Eight W4174/50 Desserts	One W4147/50 Platter
Eight W4138/50 Salad Plates	One W4153/50 Sugar
Eight W4167/50 Soup Plates	One W4154/50 Creamer

OPEN STOCK

W4179/50 — W4129/50

W4174/50

W4138/50 — W4141/50

W4167/50

			PACKING
W4179/50—	Cup		6 doz. — 26 lbs.
W4129/50—	Saucer		6 doz. — 28 lbs.
W4174/50—4 7/8″	Dessert		6 doz. — 24 lbs.
W4138/50—7 1/4″	Salad Plate		3 doz. — 26 lbs.
W4141/50—9 1/8″	Dinner Plate		3 doz. — 40 lbs.
W4167/50—7 5/8″	Soup Plate		3 doz. — 29 lbs.

W4178/50

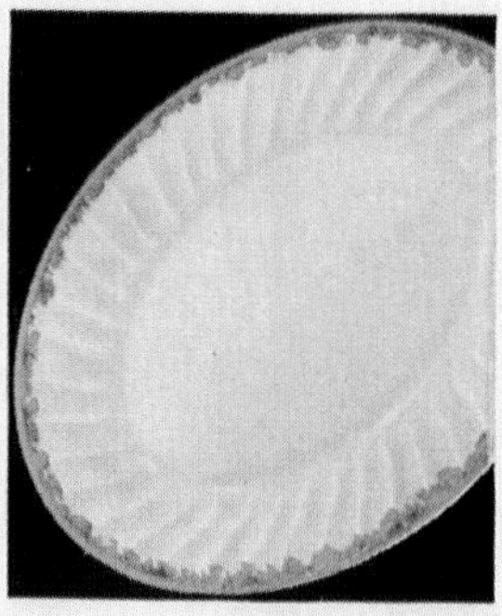

W4147/50

W4153/50 — W4154/50

W4178/50— 8 1/4″	Vegetable Bowl		1 doz. — 15 lbs.
W4147/50—12 x 9″	Platter		1 doz. — 21 lbs.
W4153/50—	Sugar		2 doz. — 10 lbs.
W4154/50—	Creamer		2 doz. — 10 lbs.

HEAT-PROOF   ANCHORWHITE — 22 K. GOLD TRIMMED

PINK Anchorglass® DINNERWARE

M4179 — M4129
M4174
M4138 — M4141 — M4146
M4167

PACKING

M4179—	8 oz. Cup		6 doz. — 25 lbs.
M4129—	5¾" Saucer		6 doz. — 32 lbs.
M4174—	4⅞" Dessert		6 doz. — 25 lbs.
M4138—	7¾" Salad Plate		3 doz. — 27 lbs.
M4141—	9⅛" Dinner Plate		3 doz. — 38 lbs.
M4146—	11" Serving Plate		1 doz. — 20 lbs.
M4167—	7⅝" Soup Plate		3 doz. — 29 lbs.

DESIGNED FOR BEAUTY — PRICED FOR EVERYDAY VOLUME SALES.

M4177 — M4178
M4143 — M4144

M4177—	7¼" Vegetable Bowl		1 doz. — 11 lbs.
M4178—	8¼" Vegetable Bowl		1 doz. — 15 lbs.
M4143—	Sugar & Cover		2 doz. — 11 lbs.
M4144—	Creamer		2 doz. — 12 lbs.

Each Piece comes with a beautiful Pink, Black and Gold
label reading "PINK HEAT-PROOF ANCHORGLASS."

See Listing of Prepacked Sets on Page 2.

— HEAT-PROOF —

FIRE-KING OVEN WARE, "SWIRL" ANCHOR HOCKING GLASS CORPORATION, 1960's-1975

Colors: white, white trimmed in gold, Jade-ite, and iridized Lustre.

Anchorwhite "Swirl" continued to be made into the early 1960's. In 1963, Hocking changed the "Swirl' into a more scalloped effect on the edge. The pattern introducing this new design was called Golden Shell which was made until late 1970's.

You can see the major difference in Golden Anniversary ("Swirl" with gold trim) and Golden Shell in the top photo on page 65. The Golden Shell plate is pictured in front of the Golden Anniversary plate. Note the distinct scalloped edge of the Golden Shell. There is a catalogue page showing the new design on page 66.

Using this new "Swirl" design, Anchor Hocking introduced a Jade-ite set in 1964. The catalogue called it an "English Regency style." To continue the confusing ways of not naming patterns, this had no real name except Jade-ite. It was listed in catalogues up until 1972.

In 1966, Lustre Shell was introduced and manufactured until the late 1970's. The soup bowl was sized upward from 6⅜" to 7⅝" with the introduction of this color. This was "Swirl" with an iridized spray like the Peach Lustre shown on pages 49 and 50. Lustre was Anchor Hocking's name for the color and shell was the design. Now why didn't they add shell to the Jade-ite and solve our name problems thirty years later?

A demitasse cup and saucer was introduced to the Lustre Shell line in 1972. Demitasse saucers are as hard to find as the cups.

On page 67 are two photographs of "Swirl" with hand painted scenes. This set was purchased from a mall in Zanesville, Ohio. I was told by the shop owner that the artist was a lady who had worked at the Fenton factory. Diagnosed with cancer, she returned home to paint dishes as her hobby. Some pieces are hand signed J. Kinney. I thought the glass was priced right for what it was and the few pieces of hand painted Pyrex in with the Anchor Hocking didn't deter me from buying it in the least little way.

	Golden Shell	Jade-ite "Shell"	Lustre Shell
Bowl, 4¾", dessert	1.50	2.25	2.50
Bowl, 6⅜", cereal	2.00	3.25	3.50
Bowl, 7⅝", soup plate	3.50	4.50	4.00
Bowl, 6⅜", soup	2.50	3.00	
Bowl, 8½", vegetable	5.00	5.50	6.50
Creamer, ftd.	3.00	5.00	5.00
Cup, 8 oz.	3.00	3.50	3.50
Cup, 3¼ oz., demitasse			6.00
Saucer, 4¾", demitasse			4.00
Plate, 7¼", salad	2.00	2.25	2.50
Plate, 10", dinner	3.00	4.00	5.00
Platter, 9½" x 13"	7.50	9.00	
Saucer, 5¾"	.50	.50	.50
Sugar, ftd.	2.50	5.00	5.00
Sugar cover	3.00	3.00	3.00

Golden Shell Dinnerware

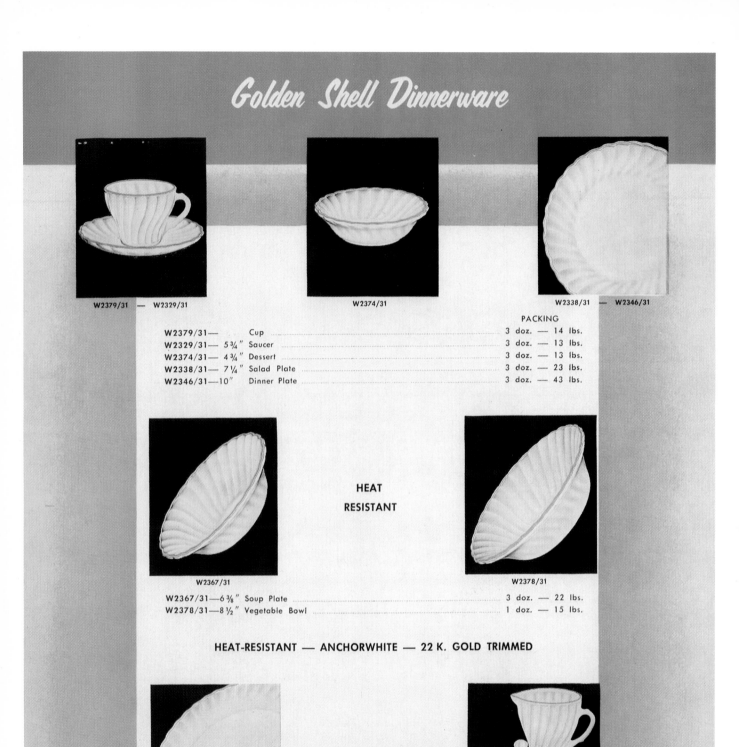

W2379/31 — W2329/31   W2374/31   W2338/31 — W2346/31

		PACKING
W2379/31—	Cup	3 doz. — 14 lbs.
W2329/31— 5¾"	Saucer	3 doz. — 13 lbs.
W2374/31— 4¾"	Dessert	3 doz. — 13 lbs.
W2338/31— 7¼"	Salad Plate	3 doz. — 23 lbs.
W2346/31—10"	Dinner Plate	3 doz. — 43 lbs.

HEAT
RESISTANT

W2367/31   W2378/31

W2367/31—6⅜" Soup Plate	3 doz. — 22 lbs.
W2378/31—8½" Vegetable Bowl	1 doz. — 15 lbs.

HEAT-RESISTANT — ANCHORWHITE — 22 K. GOLD TRIMMED

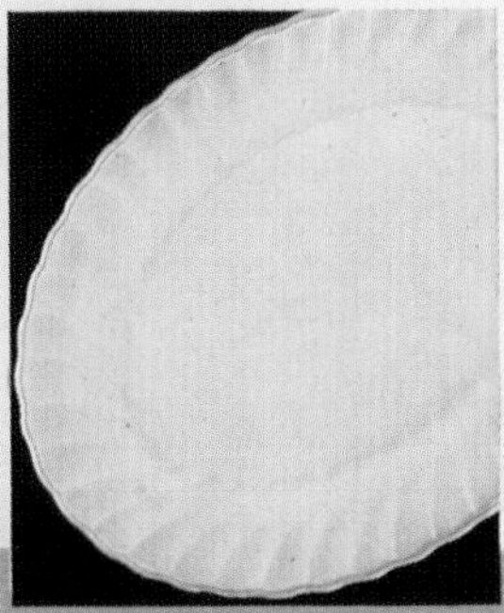

W2347/31    W2353/31 — W2354/31

W2347/31—13 x 9½" Platter	1 doz. — 22 lbs.
W2353/31— Sugar & Cover	1 doz. — 9 lbs.
W2354/31— Creamer	1 doz. — 6 lbs.

HEAT-RESISTANT

FIRE-KING OVEN WARE, WHEAT & BLUE MOSAIC ANCHOR HOCKING GLASS
CORPORATION, 1962-late 1960's

Blue Mosaic was a short lived Anchor Hocking pattern. It is shown only in a 1967 catalogue. I have been seeing a few pieces in Florida, so I hope to show you more than this platter (shown below) next time.

Wheat production began in 1962 and was one of Anchor Hocking's most productive lines of the 1960's. Like Sapphire blue Fire-King in the 1940's, everyone has seen the Wheat pattern of the 1960's!

Both the oval and round 1½ quart casseroles and the 10½" baking pan were used with candlewarmers. These candlewarmers were brass finished with walnut handles and candle. I do not price these since I have not seen a set for sale as yet.

	Wheat	Blue Mosaic		Wheat	Blue Mosaic
Bowl, 4⅝", dessert	2.00	3.50	Cup, 8 oz.	3.00	
Bowl, 6⅝", soup plate	3.50	5.50	Custard, 6 oz., low or dessert	2.00	
Bowl, 8¼", vegetable	5.50	10.00	Pan, 5" x 9", baking, w/cover	10.00	
Cake pan, 8", round	7.50		Pan, 5" x 9", deep loaf	7.50	
Cake pan, 8", square	7.50		Pan, 6½" x 10½" x 1½",		
Casserole, 1 pt., knob cover	4.50		utility baking	8.00	
Casserole, 1 qt., knob cover	7.00		Pan, 8" x 12½" x 2",		
Casserole, 1½ qt., knob cover	8.50		utility baking	10.00	
Casserole, 1½ qt., oval,			Plate, 7⅜", salad	2.00	3.00
au gratin cover	12.00		Plate, 10", dinner	3.00	4.50
Casserole, 2 qt., knob cover	10.00		Platter, 9" x 12"	8.00	12.50
Casserole, 2 qt., round,			Saucer, 5¾"	.50	.75
au gratin cover	12.00		Sugar	2.50	4.50
Creamer	3.00	5.00	Sugar cover	2.00	2.50
Cup, 5 oz., snack	2.50		Tray, 11" x 6", rectangular,		
Cup, 7½ oz.		3.50	snack	3.00	

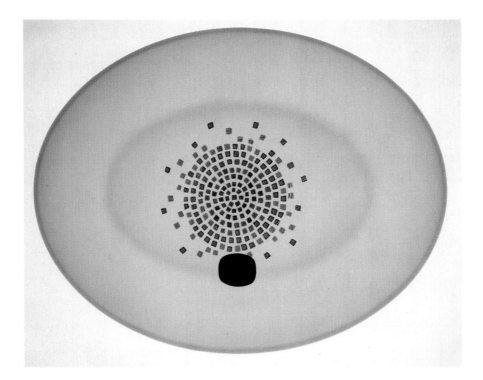

Please refer to Foreword for pricing information

W4679/65 — W4629/65   W4674/65   W4638/65 — W4646/65

		PACKING
W4679/65— 8 oz.	Cup	3 doz. — 14 lbs.
W4629/65— 5¾"	Saucer	3 doz. — 14 lbs.
W4674/65— 4⅝"	Dessert	3 doz. — 11 lbs.
W4638/65— 7⅜"	Salad Plate	3 doz. — 23 lbs.
W4646/65—10"	Dinner Plate	3 doz. — 44 lbs.

W4667/65   W4678/65

W4667/65— 6⅝"	Soup Plate	3 doz. — 25 lbs.
W4678/65— 8¼"	Vegetable Bowl	1 doz. — 14 lbs.

HEAT-RESISTANT

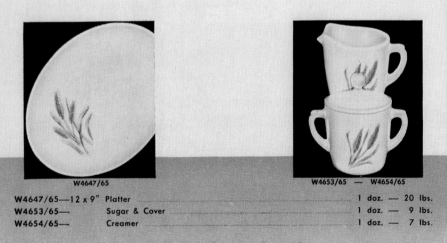

W4647/65   W4653/65 — W4654/65

W4647/65—12 x 9"	Platter	1 doz. — 20 lbs.
W4653/65—	Sugar & Cover	1 doz. — 9 lbs.
W4654/65—	Creamer	1 doz. — 7 lbs.

See Prepacked Sets on Page 13.

Wheat Anchorwhite Ovenware

W424/65   W405/65 — W406/65   W407/65 — W408/65

			PACKING
W424/65—6	oz.	Dessert or Low Custard	4 doz. — 14 lbs.
W405/65—1	Pt.	Casserole—Knob Cover	1 doz. — 16 lbs.
W406/65—1	Qt.	Casserole—Knob Cover	½ doz. — 14 lbs.
W407/65—1½	Qt.	Casserole—Knob Cover	½ doz. — 19 lbs.
W408/65—2	Qt.	Casserole—Knob Cover	½ doz. — 22 lbs.

All Covers are Clear Crystal Fire-King.

W467/65   W450/65   W452/65

W467/65—1½	Qt.	Casserole—Au Gratin Cover	½ doz. — 18 lbs.
W450/65—8"		Round Cake Pan	½ doz. — 12 lbs.
W452/65—8"		Square Cake Pan	½ doz. — 17 lbs.

GUARANTEED 2 YEARS AGAINST OVEN BREAKAGE.

To be replaced Free by dealer in exchange for broken pieces.

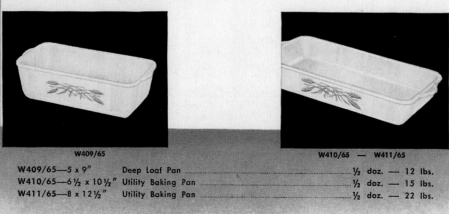

W409/65   W410/65 — W411/65

W409/65—5 x 9"	Deep Loaf Pan	½ doz. — 12 lbs.
W410/65—6½ x 10½"	Utility Baking Pan	½ doz. — 15 lbs.
W411/65—8 x 12½"	Utility Baking Pan	½ doz. — 22 lbs.

**"Fire-King" — The World's Finest Baking Ware. Also available
in Crystal, Anchorwhite and Copper-Tint.**

Wheat Ovenware Sets

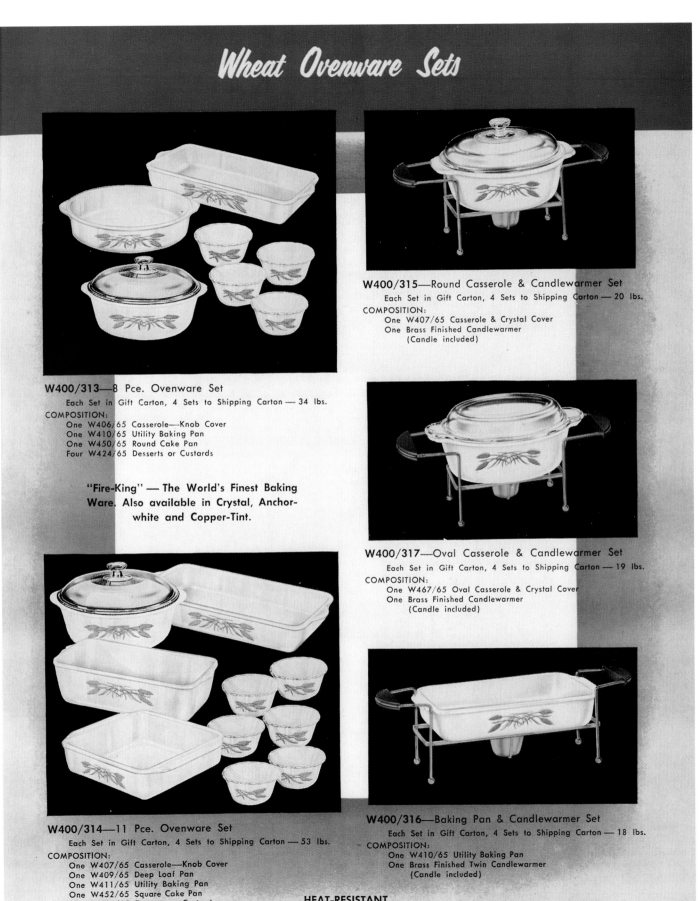

W400/313—8 Pce. Ovenware Set

Each Set in Gift Carton, 4 Sets to Shipping Carton — 34 lbs.

COMPOSITION:
One W406/65 Casserole—Knob Cover
One W410/65 Utility Baking Pan
One W450/65 Round Cake Pan
Four W424/65 Desserts or Custards

"Fire-King" — The World's Finest Baking Ware. Also available in Crystal, Anchorwhite and Copper-Tint.

W400/314—11 Pce. Ovenware Set

Each Set in Gift Carton, 4 Sets to Shipping Carton — 53 lbs.

COMPOSITION:
One W407/65 Casserole—Knob Cover
One W409/65 Deep Loaf Pan
One W411/65 Utility Baking Pan
One W452/65 Square Cake Pan
Six W424/65 Desserts or Custards

W400/315—Round Casserole & Candlewarmer Set

Each Set in Gift Carton, 4 Sets to Shipping Carton — 20 lbs.

COMPOSITION:
One W407/65 Casserole & Crystal Cover
One Brass Finished Candlewarmer
(Candle included)

W400/317—Oval Casserole & Candlewarmer Set

Each Set in Gift Carton, 4 Sets to Shipping Carton — 19 lbs.

COMPOSITION:
One W467/65 Oval Casserole & Crystal Cover
One Brass Finished Candlewarmer
(Candle included)

W400/316—Baking Pan & Candlewarmer Set

Each Set in Gift Carton, 4 Sets to Shipping Carton — 18 lbs.

COMPOSITION:
One W410/65 Utility Baking Pan
One Brass Finished Twin Candlewarmer
(Candle included)

HEAT-RESISTANT

FLORAGOLD, "LOUISA" JEANNETTE GLASS COMPANY, 1950's

Colors: iridescent, some Shell Pink, ice blue and crystal.

Floragold is often thought to be Carnival glass by "antique dealers" who do not sell much glassware. In fact, this pattern wasn't made until the early 1950's. Carnival glass is only accepted through the 1920's. Floragold was designed similar to "Louisa" which was an early Carnival glass pattern. Often the rose bowl in Carnival "Louisa" is offered for sale as Floragold which turns the confusion around the other way.

Floragold vases have gone out of sight price wise. The large tumbler, which is also not very common, was fluted and turned into a small vase. Many of these large, 15 oz. tumblers can be found in crystal selling in the $10.00 range. Crystal tumblers were sprayed with the iridized color and refired to make it stay. Evidently, many of these tumblers were never sprayed.

There are two different 5¼" comports in Floragold. One has a ruffled top and the other has a plain top. See the ruffled comport below as a pattern shot.

Perfect tops to shakers are hard to find. Because the tops were plastic, many were broken by tightening them too much. Some of these tops were made in white or brown. Only plastic tops are originals. These tops are so hard to find that $25.00 of the price of the shakers is for the tops.

There are an abundance of cups in Floragold. Cups were sold without saucers in two ways. The large bowl and the pitcher were both sold with twelve cups as "egg nog" sets for the Christmas market. Each set added to the cup production; so, today, saucers seem scarce. The 5¼" saucer has no cup ring and is the same as the sherbet plate.

Ice blue, crystal, red-yellow, Shell Pink and iridized large size comports were made in the late 1950's and into the early 1970's. See Shell Pink for this piece. All the other comports are **selling** in the $10.00 range and sitting on the shelf at $15.00 up.

	Iridescent
Ash tray/coaster, 4"	5.00
Bowl, 4½", square	5.00
Bowl, 5½", round cereal	27.50
Bowl, 5½", ruffled fruit	7.50
Bowl, 8½", square	12.50
Bowl, 9½", deep salad	32.50
Bowl, 9½", ruffled	7.50
Bowl, 12", ruffled large fruit	6.50
Butter dish and cover, ¼ lb. oblong	22.50
Butter dish and cover, round, 6¼" sq. base	37.50
Butter dish bottom	12.50
Butter dish top	25.00
Butter dish and cover, round, 5½" sq. base	600.00
Candlesticks, double branch, pr.	45.00
Candy dish, 1 handle	10.00
Candy or Cheese dish and cover, 6¾"	45.00
Candy, 5¼" long, 4 feet	6.50
Comport, 5¼", plain top	550.00
Comport, 5¼", ruffled top	650.00
Creamer	8.50
Cup	5.00
Pitcher, 64 oz.	30.00
Plate or tray, 13½"	17.50
Plate or tray, 13½", with indent	45.00
Plate, 5¼", sherbet	10.00
Plate, 8½", dinner	27.50
Platter, 11¼"	17.50
*Salt and pepper, plastic tops	45.00
Saucer, 5¼" (no ring)	10.00
Sherbet, low , footed	12.00
Sugar	6.00
Sugar lid	8.50
Tid-bit, wooden post	30.00
Tumbler, 10 oz., footed	17.50
Tumbler, 11 oz., footed	17.50
Tumbler, 15 oz., footed	65.00
Vase or celery	325.00

* Tops $12.50 each included in price

Please refer to Foreword for pricing information

FOREST GREEN ANCHOR HOCKING GLASS COMPANY CORPORATION, 1950-1967

Color: Forest Green.

Forest Green is actually the color made by Anchor Hocking and not the pattern. Originally this pattern started out using the square **Charm** blank in 1950, but the ware became better known by its color. Even the "Bubble" was called Forest Green as you can see by the catalogue on page 15.

The bottom of page 12 shows some stemware that was sold along with Bubble. These have been called "Boopie" by collectors, but they are priced about the same as the "Bubble stemware" shown on page 15 with the Forest Green Bubble. These lines are both priced below.

According to one Anchor Hocking catalogue, the Bubble stemware was actually called "Early American" line.

An oval vegetable in Forest Green has been found. This bowl is scalloped along the edges and has a swirled effect on the sides. See bowl on right of picture on page 75. Not many of these have been discovered!

For a pattern made so late, platters, 6" soup bowls and dinner plates are infrequently found. At least one listing of the 8⅜" plate was as a dinner plate, so perhaps that is why 10" dinners are so hard to find. Were they made as an after thought?

The large quantity of 4" ball ivy vases testifies to successful sales of Citronella candles which were packed in these vases. The picture shows a boxed set of two "mosquito repellent" candles which originally sold for $1.19. Having been in Florida most of the last six months makes me want to find a few cases of these for my boat dock and porch. Since the screened porch has been converted to my office facilities, I have had a slight problem with lights on after dark. Mosquitoes cover the windows on the outside until there is no more room! (Blind mosquitoes should not be able to come to light, but only the natives try to tell me they are blind!) They hit the screens and sound like rain!

One reader reports finding a box of twenty four 7 oz. tumblers in a box marked, "Clover Honey Delight, Packed by National Honey Packers Mt. Sterling Illinois."

There are several new listings to this line that I was able to obtain from Anchor Hocking's files on my last trip there. The "fancy" tumbler (Anchor Hocking designation) listed below is the one shown on the bottom of page 75 next to the vase on the left in the back.

	Green			Green			Green
Ash tray, 3½", square	3.50		Plate, 6⅝", salad	3.00		*Stem, 14 oz., iced tea	17.50
Ash tray, 4⅝", square	4.50		Plate, 8⅜", luncheon	5.00		Sugar, flat	5.50
Ash tray, 5¾", square	6.50		Plate, 10", dinner	20.00		Tumbler, 5 oz., 3½"	3.00
Ash tray, 5¾", hexagonal	7.50		Platter, 11", rectangular	25.00		Tumbler, 7 oz.	3.50
Batter bowl w/spout	12.50		Punch bowl	20.00		Tumbler, 9 oz, table	4.50
Bowl, 4¾", dessert	5.00		Punch bowl stand	20.00		Tumbler, 9 oz., fancy	5.00
Bowl, 5¼" deep	8.00		Punch cup (round)	2.00		Tumbler, 9½ oz., tall	6.00
Bowl, 6", soup	14.00		Saucer, 5⅜"	1.00		Tumbler, 10 oz., ftd., 4½"	6.00
Bowl, 6", mixing	8.50		Sherbet, flat	6.00		Tumbler, 11 oz.	6.50
Bowl, 7⅜", salad	9.50		*Stem, 3½ oz., cocktail	7.00		Tumbler, 13 oz., iced tea	7.00
Bowl, 8½", oval vegetable	25.00		*Stem, 4 oz., juice	9.00		Tumbler, 14 oz., 5"	7.00
Creamer, flat	5.50		Stem, 4½ oz., cocktail	8.00		Tumbler, 15 oz., long boy	8.00
Cup (square)	4.00		Stem, 5½ oz., juice	10.00		Tumbler, 19 oz., jumbo iced tea	12.00
Pitcher, 22 oz.	19.50		Stem, 6 oz., sherbet	7.50		Vase, 4" ivy ball	3.00
Pitcher, 36 oz.	22.50		*Stem, 6 oz., sherbert	7.00		Vase, 6⅜"	4.00
Pitcher, 86 oz., round	25.00		*Stem, 9 oz., goblet	12.00		Vase, 9"	6.00
Plate, 6¾", salad	3.00		Stem, 9½ oz., goblet	11.00			

* "Boopie"

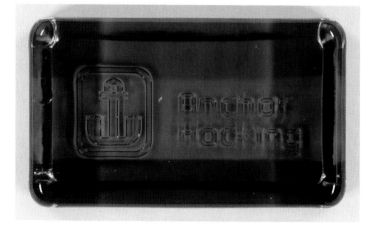

Please refer to Foreword for pricing information

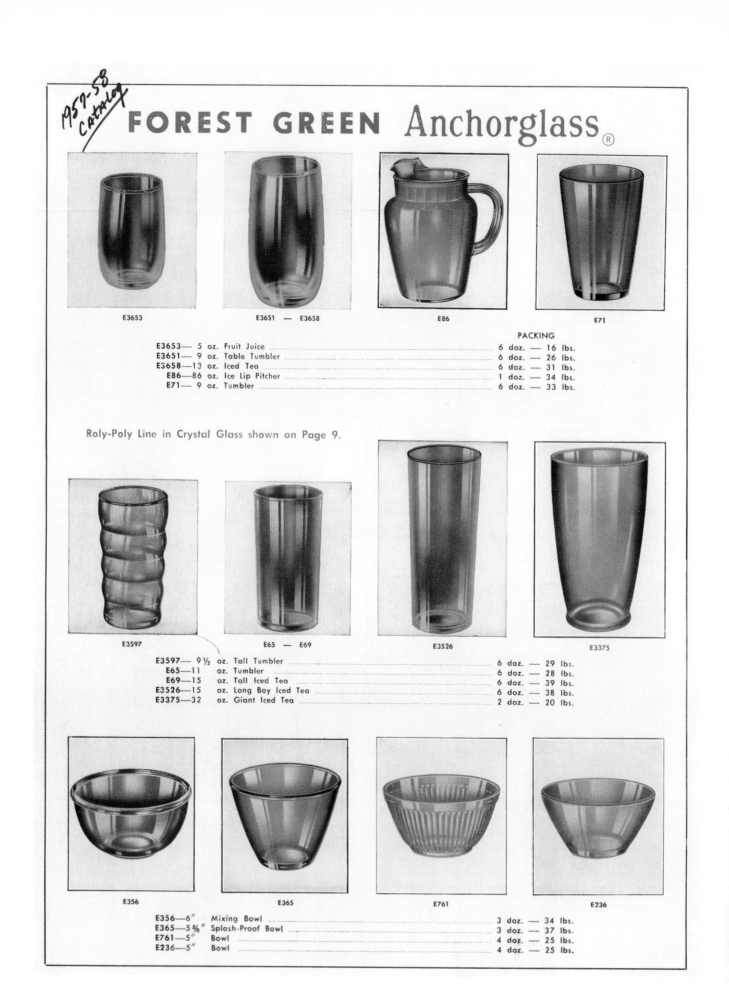

1957-58 Catalog

FOREST GREEN Anchorglass®

E3653

E3651 — E3658

E86

E71

PACKING

E3653— 5 oz. Fruit Juice	6 doz. — 16 lbs.	
E3651— 9 oz. Table Tumbler	6 doz. — 26 lbs.	
E3658—13 oz. Iced Tea	6 doz. — 31 lbs.	
E86—86 oz. Ice Lip Pitcher	1 doz. — 34 lbs.	
E71— 9 oz. Tumbler	6 doz. — 33 lbs.	

Roly-Poly Line in Crystal Glass shown on Page 9.

E3597

E65 — E69

E3526

E3375

E3597— 9 ½ oz. Tall Tumbler	6 doz. — 29 lbs.	
E65—11 oz. Tumbler	6 doz. — 28 lbs.	
E69—15 oz. Tall Iced Tea	6 doz. — 39 lbs.	
E3526—15 oz. Long Boy Iced Tea	6 doz. — 38 lbs.	
E3375—32 oz. Giant Iced Tea	2 doz. — 20 lbs.	

E356

E365

E761

E236

E356—6" Mixing Bowl	3 doz. — 34 lbs.	
E365—5 ⅝" Splash-Proof Bowl	3 doz. — 37 lbs.	
E761—5" Bowl	4 doz. — 25 lbs.	
E236—5" Bowl	4 doz. — 25 lbs.	

HARP JEANNETTE GLASS COMPANY, 1954-1957

Colors: crystal, crystal with gold trim, and cake stands in Shell Pink, pink, white and ice blue.

Another colored cake stand in Harp has been found. You can see the newly discovered iridescent one below. That brings the total to nine different cake stands in Harp.

1. Crystal with smooth rim
2. Crystal with ruffled rim
3,4. Either of above with gold trim
5. Iridescent with smooth rim
6,7,8. Ice blue, white or Shell Pink (opaque) with beads on rim and foot
9. Pink transparent

No wonder a collector can resort to collecting only Harp cake stands. There are enough different ones to keep you searching for a while. You can see the Shell Pink stand under that pattern on page 129.

Many collectors love this set to use for their bridge parties. With the ever present cake stand, cups, saucers and the 7" plates, you can make a great small table setting. The Harp cake stand is reminiscent of early 1900's glassware. Most patterns after that time had cake plates instead of a stand.

Popularity of this pattern with collectors has caused some large price increases. There is not enough of this smaller pattern to accommodate everyone.

The vase stands 7½" and not 6".

	Crystal			Crystal
Ash tray/coaster	4.50	Plate, 7"		8.50
Coaster	3.50	Saucer		3.50
Cup	9.00	**Tray, 2-handled, rectangular		27.50
*Cake stand, 9"	20.00	Vase, 7½"		15.00

* Ice blue, white, pink or Shell Pink - $25.00
** Shell Pink $45.00

HERITAGE FEDERAL GLASS COMPANY, 1940 -1955

Colors: crystal, some pink, blue, green and cobalt.

Heritage prices continue to escalate even with the reproduction problems of the bowls. Crystal creamers and 8½" berry bowls are still the most difficult of all pieces to find. The sugar turns up more frequently for some reason. Those pink, blue and green berry bowls all remain elusive. These are truly rare!

Heritage was advertised as late as 1954 in some of the women's magazines.

Crystal sets can be gathered more easily than sets of many other patterns due to the dearth of pieces. There are only ten separate pieces to find, so the limitation you have is whether to search for a six, eight or twelve place setting. Thankfully, you only have to find one creamer no matter how many place settings you collect.

Why anyone would want to remake this little pattern is beyond my comprehension. Reproductions of Heritage bowls are being marketed by McCrory's. These are being made in amber, crystal and green. Most are marked "MC" in the center. I say most because not all reports from readers have mentioned this mark. In any case, the smaller berry bowls are selling three for $1.00 and the larger for $1.59 each. The pattern on these pieces is not very good and should not fool even beginning collectors. Just compare the full designed hobs in my picture to the sparsely designed hobs on the reproductions. The green being found is much darker and closer to the avocado colored green of the 1970's than to the pretty shade of green shown here. Amber was never made originally; so, that is no problem.

Refer to Daisy for an explanation of Indiana's Heritage pattern in green.

	Crystal	Pink	Blue Green
Bowl, 5", berry	7.00	35.00	45.00
Bowl, 8½", large berry	25.00	95.00	150.00
Bowl, 10½", fruit	12.50		
Cup	6.00		
Creamer, footed	20.00		
Plate, 8", luncheon	7.50		
Plate, 9¼", dinner	10.00		
Plate, 12", sandwich	11.50		
Saucer	3.00		
Sugar, open, footed	15.00		

HOLIDAY, "BUTTONS AND BOWS" JEANNETTE GLASS COMPANY, 1947-mid 1950's

Colors: pink, iridescent; some Shell Pink, and crystal.

Beginning collectors need to know that there are three styles of cup and saucer sets. One style cup and saucer have a plain center. These are easy to match up and are shown on the left. There are two other styles of cups that have a rayed center. You can not mix these together since the base of the cup will not fit the saucer ring of the wrong type. Rayed cups have to go on rayed saucers, but you have to check these for size of the cup bottom also. One cup's base is 2" and fits a 2⅛" saucer ring. The other cup's base is 2⅜" and fits a 2½" saucer ring.

There are two styles of 10 oz. tumblers, as can be seen in the picture. The tumbler on the right is flat bottomed, while the one on the left has a small raised foot and is narrower at the bottom. There is no difference in price, but purist collectors need to know that there are variances in pieces. These are just from different moulds, but new collectors sometimes get upset with differences on the same item purchased in different places.

While we are pointing out differences, there are also two different style sherbets. The one on the right has a rayed foot while the one on the left is plain. The two sherbet plates both have 2¾" centers, but the one on the left has a "beads" effect in the center, while the one on the left has a center ring with a "diamond" effect in the center. These mould variations occur in many patterns, but it is confusing unless you know what to expect. It is all right to mix styles, but some people do not wish to do so. These confusing items are all shown on the bottom of page 79.

HOLIDAY, "BUTTONS AND BOWS" JEANNETTE GLASS COMPANY, 1947-mid 1950's

If you missed page 78, be sure to refer to it to learn about the different styles of Holiday pieces.

If you missed a previous explanation for the rarity of some of the Holiday pieces, I include it again. "Holiday seems to have suffered the same fate as Floral and Doric and Pansy. The pieces that we have difficulty in finding in these patterns were exported. Unlike the other patterns which seem to have been sent to England, Holiday was exported to the Philippines." As reported in the ninth *Collector's Encyclopedia of Depression Glass*, iced teas, soups and juices were found in abundance there. The tumblers were sent in boxes of six to be used as premiums for a well known chocolate bar.

Holiday console bowls, candlesticks and cake plates are the most difficult pieces to find outside of those pieces discussed previously. You wonder how such a lately manufactured glassware could have so many hard to find pieces! Also, Holiday seems to have been a heavily used pattern judging by all the lone butter bottoms found and the multitude of damaged pieces I have incurred as I have looked at sets over the years.

Yes, the iced tea tumblers are actually fetching that price, a far cry from the $10.00 each I paid for six for my Mom's collection in the early 1970's! That was a **big** price for any tumbler in those days.

You should also be aware in examining Holiday that the points which protrude are prone to chips, nicks and "chigger bites", an auction term that varies from place to place. Some auction houses must harbor some big chiggers! Remember, damaged glass can't be "almost" mint. The prices listed here are for mint condition glassware!

	Pink	Crystal	Iridescent
Bowl, 5⅛", berry	10.00		
Bowl, 7¾", soup	37.50		
Bowl, 8½", large berry	18.00		
Bowl, 9½", oval vegetable	15.00		
*Bowl, 10¾", console	85.00		
Butter dish and cover	32.50		
Butter dish bottom	10.00		
Butter dish top	22.50		
Cake Plate, 10½", 3 legged	80.00		
Candlesticks, 3" pr.	75.00		
Creamer, footed	7.50		
Cup, three sizes	6.00		
Pitcher, 4¾", 16 oz. milk	50.00	15.00	20.00
Pitcher, 6¾", 52 oz.	27.50		
Plate, 6", sherbet	4.00		
Plate, 9", dinner	14.00		
Plate, 13¾", chop	80.00		
Platter, 11⅜", oval	15.00		12.50
Sandwich tray, 10½"	13.00		
Saucer, 3 styles	4.00		
Sherbet, 2 styles	5.50		
Sugar	8.00		
Sugar cover	12.00		
Tumbler, 4", 10 oz., flat	17.50		
Tumbler, 4", footed, 5 oz.	30.00		10.00
Tumbler, 4¼", footed, 5¼ oz.		7.50	
Tumbler, 6", footed	120.00		

* Shell Pink $35.00

Please refer to Foreword for pricing information

IRIS, "IRIS AND HERRINGBONE" JEANNETTE GLASS COMPANY, 1928-1932; 1950's; 1970's

Colors: crystal, iridescent; some pink; recently bi-colored red/yellow and blue/green combinations and white.

Iris became one of the more difficult patterns to place in the division of my *Collector's Encyclopedia of Depression Glass* since it fits both time periods so well. I have decided to include crystal prices here this time also. Actually, crystal production goes back to 1928 for its start. However, some crystal was made in the late 1940's, 1950's and some pieces such as candy bottoms and vases as late as the early 1970's. Iridescent belongs entirely within the time frame of this book, and although I have also listed prices this time in the Depression book, next time they will only go in this book.

Realize that candy bottoms in iridescent are a product of the 1970's when Jeannette made crystal bottoms and flashed them with two-tone colors such as red/yellow or blue/green. Many of these were sold as vases and over time the colors have washed or peeled off making crystal candy bottoms. These can be distinguished by the lack of rays on the foot of the dish. The later made ones all are plain footed. By the same token, white vases were made and sprayed on the outside in green, red and blue. White vases of this vintage sell in the $8.00-10.00 range.

I said that Iris was the hottest selling crystal pattern in my the ninth *Collector's Encyclopedia of Depression Glass*, but little did I realize what an understatement that was! About the time the book came out with Iris on the cover, everyone seemed to want to collect it. There was already a short supply of many pieces because of the heavy demand from the South, Tennessee in particular, where Iris is the state flower. Suddenly, no dealer could have enough stock of this pattern, and the demand far out stripped the supply. A few dealers began to raise prices and suddenly the race was on to see who could get the highest prices. Many collectors got caught up in the frenzy, and some prices almost doubled. Things have settled down now that collectors have decided that prices are higher than they are willing to pay.

One of the contributing factors to the rise in price of iridescent pieces is the person in Pennsylvania who has discovered a way to remove the iridescence from Iris and change iridescent soup bowls ($35.00 to $45.00 in price) to crystal (which are selling in the $100.00 range). Most of the items I have seen that have been changed have a very cloudy look to the iris flowers on the pieces. It was quite an enterprising project because years ago I had been told by former glass factory workers that it could not be done!

I heard of a group of twelve iridized water goblets at a show in Springfield, Illinois, last summer; but by the time I contacted the dealer, all were sold. I still have never owned one although I have seen them in collections. This goblet and the demitasse cup and saucer are the most difficult pieces to find in the iridescent color.

The decorated red and gold Iris that keeps turning up was called "Corsage" and styled by Century in 1946. We know this because of a card attached to a 1946 "Corsage" wedding gift that a reader shared with me. Does anyone know more?

The bowls advertising "Babcock Furniture will treat you right" seem to be coming from the southern part of the country. If anyone knows where this store was or still is, let me know.

Prices for both colors will be listed in this book.

	Crystal	Iridescent		Crystal	Iridescent	Pink/ Green
Bowl, 4½", berry, beaded edge	35.00	7.50	Goblet, 4¼", 4 oz., cocktail	20.00		
Bowl, 5", ruffled, sauce	8.00	20.00	Goblet, 4¼", 3 oz., wine	15.00		
Bowl, 5", cereal	70.00		Goblet, 5¾", 4 oz.	20.00		
Bowl, 7½", soup	100.00	45.00	Goblet, 5¾", 8 oz.	20.00	95.00	
Bowl, 8", berry, beaded edge	62.50	15.00	Lamp shade, 11½"	40.00		
*Bowl, 9½", ruffled, salad	10.00	10.00	Pitcher, 9½", footed	32.50	35.00	
Bowl, 11½", ruffled, fruit	10.00	10.00	Plate, 5½", sherbet	10.00	10.00	
Bowl, 11", fruit, straight edge	45.00		Plate, 8", luncheon	50.00		
Butter dish and cover	40.00	37.50	Plate, 9", dinner	45.00	35.00	
Butter dish bottom	12.50	10.00	Plate, 11¾", sandwich	20.00	20.00	
Butter dish top	27.50	27.50	Saucer	9.00	8.00	
Candlesticks, pr.	35.00	40.00	Sherbet, 2½", footed	20.00	11.00	
Candy jar and cover	95.00		Sherbet, 4", footed	16.00		
Coaster	65.00		Sugar	9.00	8.00	75.00
Creamer, footed	9.00	10.00	Sugar cover	10.00	10.00	
Cup	12.00	11.00	Tumbler, 4", flat	82.50		
**Demitasse cup	27.50	100.00	Tumbler, 6", footed	15.00	14.00	
**Demitasse saucer	107.50	125.00	Tumbler, 6½", footed	25.00		
Fruit or nut set	40.00	45.00	Vase, 9"	22.50	20.00	95.00
Goblet, 4", wine		27.50				

*Pink - $50.00

**Ruby, Blue, Amethyst priced as Iridescent

Please refer to Foreword for pricing information

JAMESTOWN FOSTORIA GLASS COMPANY, 1958-1982

Colors: amber, amethyst, blue, brown, crystal, green, pink, and red.

    Jamestown is one of those patterns that stemware seems to be all that you see for sale. Serving pieces were not marketed for as long as the stemware, so that means that everyone is now searching for serving pieces! Not all pieces were made in each color. I have grouped the colors into three pricing groups. Many dealers do not stock the amber and brown. They have found that there is almost no demand for these colors. In the middle group, crystal is most in demand. Ruby sells almost as fast as crystal, but there is not a complete line of the Ruby.

    Note the line numbers on the stems. There are two different sizes and capacities listed for the same item. These came from two different Fostoria catalogues, and it is one of the many things that drives me to distraction when writing a book. Which figure do you use? I have included both for the purist. Either some one measured incorrectly one year or the sizes were actually changed. I have run into this in other company's catalogues, so I point this out to make you aware of why your measurements can differ from those I have listed.

	Amber/Brown	Amethyst/Crystal/Green	Blue/Pink/Ruby
Bowl, 4½", dessert #2719/421	8.00	12.50	15.00
Bowl, 10", salad #2719//211	20.00	35.00	40.00
Bowl, 10", two hndl. serving #2719/648	20.00	37.50	47.50
Butter w/cover, ¼ pound #2719/300	22.50	42.50	52.50
Cake plate, 9½", hndl. #2719/306	15.00	30.00	35.00
Celery, 9¼" #2719/360	17.50	30.00	35.00
Cream, 3½", ftd. #2719/681	10.00	15.00	22.50
Jelly w/cover, 6⅛" #2719/447	30.00	50.00	70.00
Pickle, 8⅜" #2719/540	20.00	32.50	37.50
Pitcher, 7⁵⁄₁₆", 48 oz., ice jug #2719/456	40.00	85.00	110.00
Plate, 8" #2719/550	8.00	15.00	17.50
Plate, 14", torte #2719/567	25.00	40.00	50.00
Relish, 9⅛", 2 part #2719/620	15.00	30.00	35.00
Salad set, 4 pc. (10" bowl, 14" plate w/wood fork & spoon) #2719/286	50.00	80.00	95.00
Salver, 7" high, 10" diameter #2719/630	40.00	65.00	80.00
Sauce dish w/cover, 4½" #2719/635	17.50	27.50	30.00
Shaker, 3½", w/chrome top. pr. #2719/653	25.00	35.00	45.00
Stem, 4⁵⁄₁₆", 4 oz., wine #2719/26	9.00	18.00	22.50
Stem, 4¼", 6½ oz., sherbet #2719/7	6.00	12.00	15.00
Stem, 4⅛", 7 oz., sherbet #2719/7	6.00	12.00	15.00
Stem, 5¾", 9½ oz., goblet #2719/2	9.00	18.00	20.00
Stem, 5⅞", 10 oz., goblet #2719/2	9.00	18.00	20.00
Sugar, 3½", ftd. #2719/679	10.00	15.00	22.50
Tray, 9⅜", hndl. muffin #2719/726	25.00	40.00	50.00
Tumbler, 4¼", 9 oz. #2719/73	8.00	20.00	24.00
Tumbler, 4¾", 5 oz., juice #2719/88	8.50	20.00	25.00
Tumbler, 5⅛", 12 oz. #2719/64	8.00	20.00	24.00
Tumbler, 6", 11 oz., ftd. tea #2719/63	9.00	20.00	22.50
Tumbler, 6", 12 oz., ftd. tea #2719/63	9.00	20.00	22.50

Please refer to Foreword for pricing information

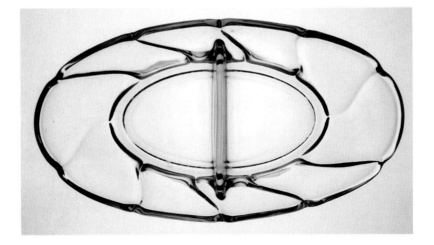

MODERNTONE PLATONITE
HAZEL ATLAS GLASS COMPANY, 1940-early 1950's

Colors: Platonite pastel, white and white decorated.

I found myself both buying and borrowing more Platonite Moderntone than I had ever done as I prepared for this book. The organization of colors was set up to show the varieties available and not necessarily to help in pricing. Because there are varying shades that make a difference in price, I chose color as the predominate factor. Children's dishes have their own section starting on page 91.

Pastel colors are light shades of blue, green, pink and yellow. Pastel blue is illustrated on the right side of the bottom of page 87; pastel green on the right at the top of page 89, pastel pink at the bottom of page 89 and pastel yellow on the right at the top of Page 90.

You may notice that there are two distinct shades of pink on the bottom of page 89. I have been assured by Moderntone collectors that this difference in shade is of no consequence to them. It bothers me to the point that I placed the lighter shades on the far right of the photograph to illustrate my point regarding color shades.

Between my Mom and a local collector, observations about Moderntone expressed here have come from over 2500 pieces of Platonite and over 1250 pieces of children's sets. That should be an adequate representation to show a few trends.

In the Pastel colors there is little difference in price range on the pieces with white interiors as opposed to those with colored interiors. My sales records show that the colored interiors are faster sellers. My wife, however, prefers the white interiors.

All bowls come with or without rims. Bowls without rims are in shorter supply, but bowls with rims tend to have inner rim roughness which "turns off" many collectors. Pastel pink 8" bowls are easier to find than other pastel colors.

To date, there is little demand for the plain white or the white trimmed in red, et cetera; however, display a piece of Blue Willow or Deco trimmed Moderntone and get out of the collector's way!

For observations about the darker colors of Platonite, turn to page 88.

	Pastel Colors	White or w/stripes	Deco/ Blue Willow
Bowl, 4¾", cream soup	6.25	3.50	15.00
Bowl, 5", berry, w/rim	4.50	2.50	9.00
Bowl, 5", berry, wo/rim	5.50		
Bowl, 5", deep cereal, w/white	7.00	3.50	
Bowl, 5", deep cereal, wo/white	8.00		
Bowl, 8", w/rim	*12.00	5.50	20.00
Bowl, 8", wo/rim	*15.00		
Bowl, 8¾", large berry		6.50	22.50
Creamer	4.50	3.00	15.00
Cup	3.00	2.00	17.50
Mug, 4", 8 oz.		7.50	
Plate, 6¾", sherbet	4.00	1.75	7.50
Plate, 8⅞", dinner	5.00	2.50	17.50
Plate, 10½", sandwich	10.00	6.00	
Platter, 11", oval		10.00	20.00
Platter, 12", oval	**12.00	7.50	25.00
Salt and pepper, pr.	15.00	12.50	
Saucer	1.50	1.00	3.00
Sherbet	4.00	2.25	8.50
Sugar	4.50	3.00	15.00
Tumbler, 9 oz.	8.00		

*Pink $8.50
* *Yellow $8.00

Please refer to Foreword for pricing information

MODERNTONE PLATONITE (Cont.)

HAZEL ATLAS GLASS COMPANY, 1940-early 1950's

Colors: dark Platonite fired-on colors.

If you collect pastel Platonite you will have only a few problems in finding some of the pieces; but if you collect what is known as the darker or late colors, you will need lots of patience or plenty of time to look. There is so little of this available, you had better buy it when you see it!

I am dividing colors into two distinct price groups based upon availability. The first group consist of cobalt blue, turquoise green, "lemon" yellow and orange. These can be found pictured as: cobalt (bottom page 87 left), turquoise (top page 89 left), "lemon" (top page 90 left) and orange (bottom page 90). All of these colors can be collected in sets with difficulty, but they can be found eventually. All can be found with white or colored interiors.

Collecting a set of any of the other colors, i.e. Chartreuse, Burgundy, Green, Gray, "rust" or "gold" is another matter. As far as I can determine, none of the following can be found on white, thus no white interiors are found. These colors are all shown at the top of page 91 except for Chartreuse which can only be seen in the child's set on the left at the bottom of page 93. The sugar, creamer and cup are Chartreuse in that set. Colors shown on the top of page 91 are as follows: Burgundy Green, Gray, "rust" and "gold." Collectors have called the Green incorrectly "forest green" and the Burgundy "maroon." I have also heard the "gold" referred to as "butterscotch" which is a better name as far as I am concerned. As with the pink, some collectors may consider the "gold" merely a variation of the "lemon" yellow and not a separate color. In any case, you have a challenge on your hands if you pick any of these colors to collect!

	Cobalt/Turquoise Lemon/Orange	Burgundy/Chartreuse Green/Gray/Rust/Gold
Bowl, 4¾", cream soup	9.00	
Bowl, 5", berry, w/rim	10.00	
Bowl, 5", berry, wo/rim	7.00	10.00
Bowl, 5", deep cereal, w/white	10.00	
Bowl, 5", deep cereal, wo/white		12.50
Bowl, 8", w/rim	25.00	
Bowl, 8", wo/rim	25.00	30.00
Creamer	7.50	9.00
Cup	5.00	6.50
Plate, 6¾", sherbet	5.00	7.00
Plate, 8⅞" dinner	8.50	10.00
Plate, 10½" sandwich	17.50	
Platter, 12" oval	17.50	25.00
Salt and pepper, pr.	20.00	
Saucer	4.50	5.50
Sherbet	6.50	8.50
Sugar	7.50	9.00
Tumbler, 9 oz.	10.00	20.00

MODERNTONE "LITTLE HOSTESS PARTY DISHES,"
HAZEL ATLAS GLASS COMPANY, early 1950's

Prices have soared on all these different colored LITTLE HOSTESS PARTY DISHES. Even Cathy had a set with turquoise tea pot left over from her childhood! She received her set as a premium with Big Top Peanut Butter. (See top page 93).

Notice that the child's cups were also sold as souvenir items. This particular one shown in with the pink and black is from Canada.

No sooner do you say something in one book and events change it. I said that Burgundy tea pots were more difficult to find than turquoise in the last *Collector's Encyclopedia of Depression Glass* and the next few months proved that wrong as Burgundy after Burgundy tea pot came out of hiding.

LITTLE HOSTESS PARTY SET
Pink/Black/White (top 92)

Cup, ¾", bright pink	12.00
Saucer, 3⅞", black	10.00
Plate, 5¼", black, bright pink	12.50
Creamer, 1¾", bright pink	15.00
Sugar, 1¾", bright pink	15.00
Tea pot, 3½", bright pink	55.00
Tea pot lid, black	55.00
Set, 16 piece	275.00

LITTLE HOSTESS PARTY SET
Lemon/Beige/Pink/Aqua
(bottom 92)

Cup, ¾", bright pink/aqua/lemon	12.00
Saucer, 3⅞", same	10.00
Plate, 5¼", same	12.50
Creamer, 1¾", pink	15.00
Sugar, 1¾", pink	15.00
Tea pot, 3½", brown	55.00

Tea pot lid, lemon	55.00
Set, 16 piece	275.00

LITTLE HOSTESS PARTY SET
Gray/Rust/Gold
Turquoise(top 93)

Cup, ¾", Gray,rust	7.00
Cup, ¾", gold, turquoise	9.00
Saucer, 3⅞", all four colors	5.00
Plate, 5¼", same	7.50
Creamer, 1¾", rust	10.00
Sugar, 1¾", rust	10.00
Tea pot, 3½", turquoise	45.00
Tea pot lid, turquoise	45.00
Set, 16 piece	195.00

LITTLE HOSTESS PARTY SET
Green/Gray/Chartreuse/
Burgundy (bottom 93 left)

Cup, ¾", Green, Gray, Chartreuse	7.00

Cup, ¾", Burgundy	9.00
Saucer, 3⅞", Green, Gray, Chartreuse	4.50
Plate, 5¼", Burgundy	6.00
Creamer, 1¾", Chartreuse	10.00
Sugar, 1¾", Chartreuse	10.00
Tea pot, 3½", Burgundy	35.00
Tea pot lid, Burgundy	40.00
Set, 16 piece	145.00

LITTLE HOSTESS PARTY SET
Pastel pink/green/blue
yellow (bottom 93 right)

Cup, ¾", all four colors	5.50
Saucer, 3⅞", same	3.00
Plate, 5¼", same	5.50
Creamer, 1¾", pink	10.00
Sugar, 1¾", pink	10.00
Set, 14 piece	75.00

Please refer to Foreword for pricing information

MOONSTONE ANCHOR HOCKING GLASS CORPORATION, 1941-1946

Colors: crystal with opalescent hobnails and some green with opalescent hobnails.

Moonstone was the original dividing point for this book. Unfortunately, there are some patterns with rather vague dates of manufacture and some overlapping time periods which do not make the dividing line of 1940 quite as exacting as I would have liked. In any case Moonstone was a truly 1940's glassware and I hope you enjoy seeing the original photograph of a J. J. Newberry store window display on page 96. I normally would not use a black and white photo, but I felt this was too good to pass!

Collectors can not easily find the 5½" berry bowl shown in the foreground on the right in my photo. There are none of those in the store display either! How do you like an original photograph of a storefront display of Moonstone? Of course goblets and cup and saucers are also missing in the store window and they are easy to find today. The ruffled 5½" bowls are more readily found, but even they are not abundant. Have you noticed that all size plates have disappeared into collections?

Given the odd pieces shown in the bottom photograph with Moonstone stickers, it seems that Moonstone may have referred more to the process of white edging than to the actual pattern.

The green was issued under the name "Ocean Green" and was made in sets containing goblets, cups, saucers, plates, creamer and sugars. Note the two pieces shown are different than the standard line that was shown in the catalogue pages on Page 97. I wonder if the pink had a name.

Moonstone collectors buy Fenton Hobnail pitchers and tumblers to go with their sets since there are no pitchers or tumblers in Moonstone.

There are no Moonstone shakers. These, too, are Fenton. There is no Moonstone cologne bottle. It, also, is Fenton. The Fenton pieces go well with Moonstone; and, if you would like additional pieces that are similar to your pattern, by all means buy these! The hobs on the Fenton are more pointed than on Moonstone, but the colors match very well.

	Opalescent Hobnail
Bowl, 5½", berry	15.00
Bowl, 5½", crimped, dessert	8.00
Bowl, 6½", crimped, handled	9.00
Bowl, 7¾", flat	11.00
Bowl, 7¾", divided relish	9.50
Bowl, 9½", crimped	17.50
Bowl, cloverleaf	12.00
Candle holder, pr.	15.00
Candy jar and cover, 6"	22.50
Cigarette jar and cover	20.00
Creamer	7.00
Cup	7.00
Goblet, 10 oz.	17.50
Heart bonbon, one handle	11.00
Plate, 6¼", sherbet	5.00
Plate, 8", luncheon	12.50
Plate, 10", sandwich	20.00
Puff box and cover, 4¾", round	20.00
Saucer (same as sherbet plate)	5.00
Sherbet, footed	6.50
Sugar, footed	7.00
Vase, 5½", bud	10.00

Please refer to Foreword for pricing information

95

Opalescent "MOONSTONE" Glassware

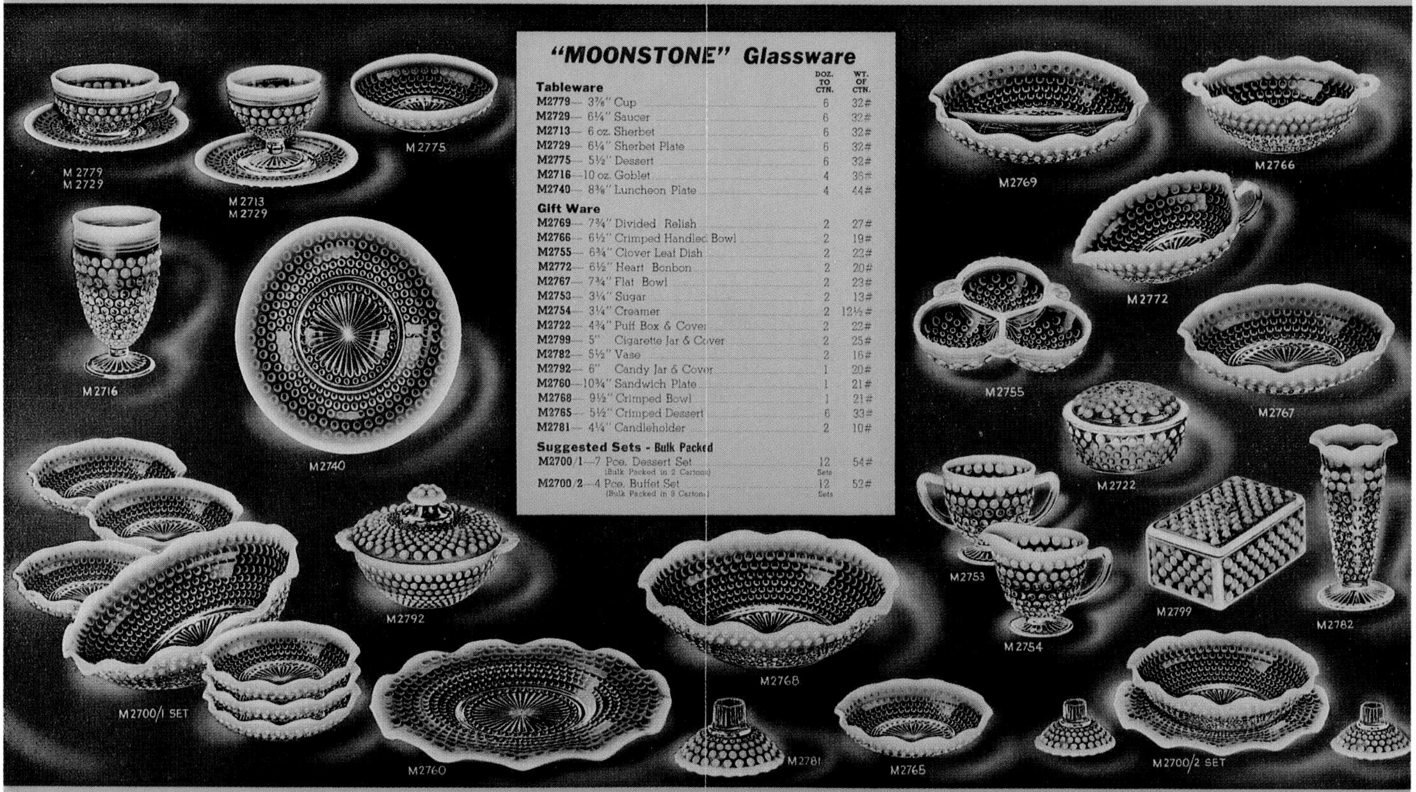

"MOONSTONE" Glassware

Tableware	DOZ. TO CTN.	WT. OF CTN.
M2779— 3⅞" Cup	6	32#
M2729— 6¼" Saucer	6	32#
M2713— 6 oz. Sherbet	6	32#
M2729— 6¼" Sherbet Plate	6	32#
M2775— 5½" Dessert	6	32#
M2716—10 oz. Goblet	4	36#
M2740— 8⅜" Luncheon Plate	4	44#
Gift Ware		
M2769— 7¾" Divided Relish	2	27#
M2766— 6½" Crimped Handled Bowl	2	19#
M2755— 6¾" Clover Leaf Dish	2	22#
M2772— 6½" Heart Bonbon	2	20#
M2767— 7¾" Flat Bowl	2	23#
M2753— 3¼" Sugar	2	13#
M2754— 3¼" Creamer	2	12½#
M2722— 4¾" Puff Box & Cover	2	22#
M2799— 5" Cigarette Jar & Cover	2	25#
M2782— 5½" Vase	2	16#
M2792— 6" Candy Jar & Cover	1	20#
M2760—10¾" Sandwich Plate	1	21#
M2768— 9½" Crimped Bowl	1	21#
M2765— 5½" Crimped Dessert	6	33#
M2781— 4¼" Candleholder	2	10#
Suggested Sets - Bulk Packed		
M2700/1—7 Pce. Dessert Set (Bulk Packed in 2 Cartons)	12 Sets	54#
M2700/2—4 Pce. Buffet Set (Bulk Packed in 3 Cartons)	12 Sets	52#

Now Available at Low Prices

MOROCCAN AMETHYST HAZEL WARE, DIVISION OF CONTINENTAL CAN, 1960's

Color: amethyst.

Moroccan Amethyst is the **color** that is found on several styles and shapes of this Hazel Ware glass. Like Anchor Hocking's Forest Green and Royal Ruby, it was the color that was important and not shape of the pieces. Pattern took second place to color again!

There are all kinds of new pieces being found in this as you can see by the expanded listing. "The Magic Hour" 4 pc. cocktail set features a clock showing six o' clock and says "yours" on one side and "mine" on the other. In this boxed set are two 2½", 4 oz. tumblers and a spouted cocktail with glass stirrer to make up the four pieces. You can see this set pictured on the top of page 101.

The **four** stemmed pieces shown have all been found with Moroccan Amethyst labels so there is no question as to their inclusion in our list. There may be another size in this design. I have not found any other sizes of crinkled bottom design tumblers other than the 11 oz. Surely there are other sizes available. That is one of the fun things about collecting a pattern for which I have not found a catalogue listing. You may find new pieces not listed. All I ask is that you send me a picture and the measurements!

I am still amazed to see people paying $15.00 for iced tea tumblers that we sold at our first garage sale in 1967 for less than a quarter each. We sold these, which had been wedding gifts in 1964, because the top heavy tumblers were a nuisance with small kids. Not only were they top heavy but when they did turn over, they rolled, spewing the contents in all directions!

You will find two and three tier tid bits made out of many different pieces in this pattern including bowls, plates and ash trays. The combinations used are almost endless.

You will find these same shaped pieces in blue and crystal. The blue pieces have labels identifying them as "Capri" (page 18-19), but I have not seen a label on the crystal to get a name for it. These colors have also become collectible! So be on the lookout for them.

	Amethyst
Ash tray, ¾", triangular	5.00
Ash tray, 3¼", round	5.00
Ash tray, 6⅞", triangular	9.00
Ash tray, 8", square	12.50
Bowl, 4¾", fruit, octagonal	6.00
Bowl, 5¾", deep, square	9.00
Bowl, 6", round	10.00
Bowl, 7¾", oval	15.00
Bowl, 7¾", rectangular	13.00
Bowl, 7¾", rectangular w/metal handle	14.00
Bowl, 10¾"	25.00
Candy w/lid short	27.50
Candy w/lid tall	27.50
Chip and dip, 10¾" & 5¾" bowls in metal holder	35.00
Cocktail w/stirrer, 6¼", 16 oz., w/lip	25.00
Cocktail shaker w/lid	22.50
Cup	5.00
Goblet, 4", 4½ oz., wine	9.00
Goblet, 4¼", 7½ oz., sherbet	7.00
Goblet, 4⅜", 5½ oz., juice	8.50
Goblet, 5½", 9 oz., water	10.00
Ice bucket, 6"	27.50
Plate, 5¾"	4.00
Plate, 7¼", salad	6.00
Plate, 9¾", dinner	7.50
Plate, 10", fan shaped, snack w/cup rest	7.50
Plate, 12", sandwich, w/metal handle	10.00
Saucer	1.00
Tumbler, 4 oz., juice, 2½"	7.50
Tumbler, 8 oz., old fashion, 3¼"	12.50
Tumbler, 9 oz., water	10.00
Tumbler, 11 oz., water, crinkled bottom, 4¼"	11.50
Tumbler, 11 oz., water, 4⅝"	11.00
Tumbler, 16 oz., iced tea, 6½"	15.00
Vase, 8½", ruffled	35.00

Please refer to Foreword for pricing information

NAVARRE, (Plate Etching #327) FOSTORIA GLASS COMPANY, 1937-1982

Colors: crystal, blue, pink and rare in green.

Since the biggest distribution of this pattern was after the 1930's, I have chosen to include it in this book. Many of the hardest to find pieces were made near the end of Fostoria's reign in the glass making world. Most of these pieces were signed "Fostoria" although some only carried a sticker. Some factory seconds that were sold through the outlet stores were not signed.

Navarre is extremely popular on the West Coast. Prices there are higher; originally, retail prices in the West were higher due to shipping costs. I have added the later pieces of Navarre as well as the colors. You can see a 1982 catalogue sheet on page 105 which will display many of these pieces. You will find that putting together a set of Navarre will be challenging, but well worth the effort of doing it!

	Crystal	Blue/Pink		Crystal	Blue/Pink
Bell, dinner	35.00	65.00	Plate, #2440, 10½" oval cake	45.00	
Bowl, #2496, 4", square, hndl.	10.00		Plate, #2496, 14", torte	55.00	
Bowl, #2496, 4⅜", hndl.	11.00		Plate, #2464, 16", torte	75.00	
Bowl, #869, 4½", finger	35.00		Relish, #2496, 6", 2 part, square	30.00	
Bowl, #2496, 4⅝", tri-cornered	14.00		Relish, #2496, 10" x 7½", 3 part	45.00	
Bowl, #2496, 5", hndl., ftd.	17.50		Relish, #2496, 10", 4 part	50.00	
Bowl, #2496, 6", square, sweetmeat	16.00		Relish, #2419, 13¼", 5 part	75.00	
Bowl, #2496, 6¼", 3 ftd., nut	17.50		Salt & pepper, #2364, 3¼", flat, pr.	50.00	
Bowl, #2496, 7⅜", ftd., bonbon	25.00		Salt & pepper, #2375, 3½", ftd., pr.	85.00	
Bowl, #2496, 10", oval, floating garden	45.00		Salad dressing bottle, #2083, 6½"	275.00	
Bowl, #2496, 10½", hndl., ftd.	60.00		Sauce dish, #2496, div. mayo., 6½"	35.00	
Bowl, #2470½, 10½", ftd.	50.00		Sauce dish, #2496, 6½" x 5¼"	100.00	
Bowl, #2496, 12", flared	55.00		Sauce dish liner, #2496, 8", oval	25.00	
Bowl, #2545, 12½", oval, "Flame"	50.00		Saucer, #2440	5.00	
Candlestick, #2496, 4"	17.50		Stem, #6106, ¾ oz., cordial, 3⅞"	42.50	
Candlestick, #2496, 4½", double	30.00		Stem, #6106, 3¼ oz., wine, 5½"	33.50	
Candlestick, #2472, 5", double	40.00		Stem, #6106, 3½ oz., cocktail, 6"	24.50	
Candlestick, #2496, 5½"	25.00		Stem, #6106, 4 oz., oyster cocktail, 3⅝"	25.00	
Candlestick, #2496, 6", triple	40.00		Stem, #6106, 4½ oz., claret, 6"	35.00	42.50
Candlestick, #2545, 6¾", double, "Flame"	45.00		Stem, #6106, 5 oz., continental		
Candlestick, #2482, 6¾", triple	40.00		champagne, 8⅛"	37.50	47.50
Candy, w/cover, #2496, 3 part	95.00		Stem, #6106, 6 oz., cocktail/sherry, 6³⁄₁₆"	32.50	
Celery, #2440, 9"	25.00		Stem, #6106, 6 oz., low sherbet, 4⅜"	22.00	
Celery, #2496, 11"	35.00		Stem, #6106, 6 oz., saucer champagne, 5⅝"	23.50	27.50
Comport, #2496, 3¼", cheese	25.00		Stem, #6106, 6½ oz., large claret, 6½"	35.00	42.50
Comport, #2400, 4½"	27.50		Stem, #6106, 10 oz., water, 7⅝"	27.50	35.00
Comport, #2496, 4¾"	27.50		Stem, #6106, 15 oz., brandy inhaler, 5½"	45.00	
Cracker, #2496, 11" plate	40.00		Stem, #6106, 16 oz., magnum, 7¼"	55.00	65.00
Creamer, #2440, 4¼", ftd.	19.00		Sugar, #2440, 3⅝", ftd.	17.50	
Creamer, #2496, individual	15.00		Sugar, #2496, individual	15.00	
Cup, #2440	17.50		Syrup, #2586, Sani-cut, 5½"	225.00	
Ice bucket, #2496, 4⅜" high	75.00		Tid bit, #2496, 8¼", 3 ftd., turned up edge	20.00	
Ice bucket, #2375, 6" high	125.00		Tray, #2496½, 6½" for ind. sugar/creamer	20.00	
Mayonnaise, #2375, 3 piece	65.00		Tumbler, #6106, 5 oz., ftd., juice, 4⅝"	22.00	
Mayonnaise, #2496½, 3 piece	65.00		Tumbler, #6106, 10 oz., ftd., water, 5⅜"	22.50	
Pickle, #2496, 8"	25.00		Tumbler, #6106, 12 oz., flat, highball, 4⅞"	35.00	
Pickle, #2440, 8½"	27.50		Tumbler, #6106, 13 oz., flat,		
Pitcher, #5000, 48 oz., ftd.	295.00		double old fashioned, 3⅝"	37.50	
Plate, #2440, 6", bread/butter	10.00		Tumbler, #6106, 13 oz., ftd., tea, 5⅞"	27.50	32.50
Plate, #2440, 7½", salad	14.50		Vase, #4108, 5"	65.00	
Plate, #2440, 8½", luncheon	17.50		Vase, #4121, 5"	70.00	
Plate, #2440, 9½", dinner	35.00		Vase, #4128, 5"	70.00	
Plate, #2496, 10", hndl., cake	45.00		Vase, #2470, 10", ftd.	125.00	

Please refer to Foreword for pricing information

Navarre

All items in the delicately etched Navarre Pattern are available in Crystal. Some items are not available in Blue. For specific information please refer to the Fostoria Price List.

Multi-Purpose Navarre Magnums

Color Key:
NA01/Crystal
NA02/Blue

Navarre Blue Goblet

Wilma Blue — Goblet
Wilma Crystal — Goblet
Navarre Crystal — Goblet
Low Dessert/Champagne
High Dessert/Champagne

Large Claret
Claret
Cordial
Magnum
Continental Champagne

Bell
7 in. Plate
8 in. Plate
Double Old Fashioned
High Ball

Luncheon Goblet/Ice Tea
Footed Juice
Brandy Inhaler
Cocktail/Sherry

1

105

NEWPORT, "HAIRPIN" HAZEL ATLAS GLASS COMPANY, 1940-early 1950's

Colors: Platonite white and fired-on colors.

Newport is another pattern that Hazel Atlas made in the late 1930's in several transparent colors which splits this listing in both this book and *The Collector's Encyclopedia of Depression Glass*. Hazel Atlas continued making Platonite until the early 1950's.

The "Platonite" white and white with fired on colors was a popular line for Hazel Atlas. Notice the white edge on the fired-on pink plate in the rear. The edge and back of this plate is white. The pink and other colors are decorating only the top edge. The turquoise blue bowl is solid color without the white bottom you might expect.

The white shaker shown here is often used by Petalware collectors for shakers in their set since there are no shakers in that MacBeth-Evans set. It is amazing how many people have been fooled into thinking these shakers really are Petalware.

The white color comes in two distinct shades. One is very translucent and the other is a flat white similar to what many collectors know as milk glass.

If you have pieces not listed in Platonite, please let me know.

	White	Fired-on colors
Bowl, 4¾", berry	3.00	5.00
Bowl, 4¾", cream soup	5.00	8.00
Bowl, 8¼, large berry	9.00	12.00
Cup	3.00	5.00
Creamer	4.00	7.00
Plate, 6", sherbet	1.00	1.50
Plate, 8½", luncheon	2.50	4.00
Plate, 11½", sandwich	8.00	12.00
Platter, 11¾", oval	10.00	15.00
Salt and pepper, pr.	17.50	20.00
Saucer	.75	1.00
Sherbet	3.00	5.00
Sugar	4.00	7.00

OVIDE, incorrectly dubbed "NEW CENTURY" HAZEL ATLAS GLASS COMPANY, 1930-1950's

Colors: Green, black, white platonite trimmed and fired-on colors in 1950's.

Ovide is another Hazel Atlas pattern that started in the Depression era, but did not conclude being made until the 1950's. The photo on the right shows pastel banded Platonite that was used in many restaurants and competed with Anchor Hocking's Jade-ite restaurant ware line. So far, there has been little collector interest in the Platonite with pastel colored bands around the edges. More often, this economically priced glassware is being gathered up to use as everyday dishes. I'm told that it works well in both the microwave and the dishwasher. Those two facts alone will attract more buyers. If it doesn't go in the dishwasher, it is not allowed in our kitchen!

The bottom of page 108 shows both desirable lines in this pattern. I included this photo because a reader told me that the Goose decorated set was a wedding present in 1942. The Goose line was already photographed with the Art Deco decorations when I received that information. Therefore, this time the Art Deco will also be priced here. After this, it will only be in *The Collector's Encyclopedia of Depression Glass*. I still have only seen one Deco sugar and creamer priced for sale in all my travels. I purchased those for future pictures, but I have been unable to purchase a set like the one I borrowed to photograph!

One of the difficulties in ordering glass through the mail is miscommunication between buyer and seller. I purchased an eighteen piece set of dark "Moderntone" colors through the mail several years ago. The box is photographed on the bottom of 109 and the contents are shown at the top of the page. (The ash tray set was purchased separately). By the time I phoned the lady again and mailed the box back, I would have lost several dollars in the transaction; so I kept the box never realizing that some day it would come in handy as reference material. Evidently, **MODERNTONE** referred to the colors and not the pattern. In any case, the box says that it includes an eighteen piece breakfast set in Burgundy, Chartreuse, Green and Gray. This will cause some confusion in Moderntone (the pattern) colors because these are real color designations by Hazel Atlas and not colors commonly known to collectors. They have always called this color green forest or dark green. We will see what happens to tradition juxtaposed with reality.

Prices can be found on the top of page 108.

OVIDE, incorrectly dubbed "NEW CENTURY" (Cont.)

	White w/trims	Decorated White	Fired-on Colors	Art Deco
Ash tray, square			3.75	
Bowl, 4¾", berry	3.00	6.00	5.00	
Bowl, 5½", cereal, deep		12.00		
Bowl, 8", large berry			17.50	
Creamer	4.00	15.00	5.00	75.00
Cup	3.00	12.00	4.00	45.00
Plate, 6", sherbet	1.00	2.25		
Plate, 8", luncheon	2.00	12.50	3.50	40.00
Plate, 9", dinner	3.00			
Platter, 11"	7.00	22.50		
Refrigerator stacking set, 4 pc.		45.00		
Salt and pepper, pr.	12.50			
Saucer	.50	2.25		15.00
Sherbet	5.00	1.50		40.00
Sugar, open	4.00	15.00	5.00	75.00
Tumbler		16.00		75.00

PANEL GRAPE (PATTERN #1881) WESTMORELAND GLASS COMPANY, 1950-1970's

Colors: white and white w/decorations.

Panel Grape was one of Westmoreland's most successful patterns. When introduced in 1950, the few pieces made quickly gave way to more until over a hundred pieces were made. Several dealers from both the East and West coasts helped in pricing this particular pattern that I have sold little of in my shop. I have bought and sold older glass for years and it is difficult to change one's ways.

Most of these listings were provided by a friend, and the catalogue pages shown on pages 113-115 are from a 1973 catalogue. Note the birds, flowers and fruit decorations. Many non-collectors have these hanging on walls, just because they like them. It is one of those patterns you either love or hate. Some people are turned off by white milk glass and if this is not your "thing," there are plenty of other patterns in this time period to suit your fancy.

	White, and w/decorations		White, and w/decorations
Appetizer set, 3 pc. (9" relish/round fruit cocktail/ladle)	60.00	Celery or spooner, 6"	37.50
Basket, 6½", oval	22.50	Cheese or old fashioned butter, 7", round w/cover	65.00
Basket, 8"	75.00	Chocolate box, 6½", w/cover	35.00
Bottle, 5 oz., toilet	60.00	Compote, 4½", crimped	17.50
Bottle, oil or vinegar, w/stopper, 2 oz.	20.00	Compote, 7" covered, ftd.	25.00
Bowl base, 5" (used w/12"/12½" lipped/10" rnd bowls & epergnes)	50.00	Compote, 7" w/cover	22.00
Bowl, 6½" x 12½", 3⅛" high	100.00	Compote, 9" ftd., crimped	75.00
Bowl, 6½", oval	22.50	Condiment set, 5 pc. (oil and vinegar, salt and pepper on 9" oval tray)	85.00
Bowl, 8", cupped	37.50	Creamer, 6½ oz.	12.50
Bowl, 9", ftd., 6" high	45.00	Creamer, individual	10.00
Bowl, 9", ftd., w/cover	65.00	Creamer, large (goes w/lacy edge sugar)	15.00
Bowl, 9", lipped	50.00	Creamer, small	9.00
Bowl, 9", lipped, ftd.	50.00	Cup, coffee	12.00
Bowl, 9", square, w/cover	32.50	Cup, punch	10.00
Bowl, 9½", bell shape	50.00	Decanter, wine	125.00
Bowl, 9½", ftd., bell shaped	45.00	Dresser set, 4 pc. (2)5 oz. toilet bottles, puff box and 13½" oval tray	195.00
Bowl, 10", oval	35.00	Egg plate, 12"	52.50
Bowl, 10½", round	75.00	Egg tray, 10", metal center handle	25.00
Bowl, 11", oval, ftd.	50.00	Epergne set, 2 pc. (9" lipped bowl/8½" epergne vase)	75.00
Bowl, 11½", oval, ruffled edge	50.00	Epergne set, 2 pc. (12" epergne lipped bowl/8½" epergne vase)	160.00
Bowl, 12", lipped	100.00		
Bowl, 12" ftd., banana	87.50	Epergne set, 2 pc. (14" flared bowl/8½" epergne vase)	200.00
Bowl, 12½", bell shape	110.00		
Bowl, 13", punch	250.00	Epergne set, 3 pc. (12" epergne lipped bowl/5"bowl base/8½" epergne vase)	210.00
Bowl, 14", shallow, round	135.00		
Bowl, ftd., ripple top	27.50	Epergne set, 3 pc. (14" flared bowl/5"bowl base/8½" epergne vase)	275.00
Bowl, rose cupped and ftd., 4"	17.50		
Butter w/cover, ¼" pound	27.50	Flower pot	45.00
Cake salver, 10½"	42.50	Fruit cocktail w/6"sauce plate, bell shape	20.00
Cake salver, 11", round ftd., w/skirt	85.00	Fruit cocktail w/6"sauce plate, round	22.50
Canape set, 3 pc. (12½" canape tray/3½" cocktail/ladle)	115.00	Ivy ball	45.00
Candelabra, 3 lite, ea.	200.00	Jardiniere, 5", cupped and ftd.	22.50
Candle holder, 4", octagonal, pr.	25.00	Jardiniere, 5", straight sided	22.50
Candle holder, 5" w/colonial hndl.	27.50	Jardiniere, 6½", cupped and ftd.	32.50
Candle holder, 8", 2 lite (4 of these form a circular center piece)	25.00	Jardiniere, 6½", straight sided	32.50
Candy jar, 3 ftd., w/cover	30.00	Jelly, 4½", covered	22.50
Candy jar, 6½", w/cover	20.00	Ladle, punch	55.00
Canister, 7"	100.00	Marmalade, w/ladle	65.00
Canister, 9½"	125.00	Mayonnaise set, 3 pc. (round fruit cocktail/6" sauce plate/ladle)	30.00
Canister, 11"	150.00	Mayonnaise, 4", ftd.	25.00

Please refer to Foreword for pricing information

PANEL GRAPE (PATTERN #1881) (Cont.)

	White, and w/decorations		White, and w/decorations
Napkin ring	15.00	Soap dish	65.00
Nappy, 4½", round	12.00	Stem, 2 oz. cordial or wine goblet	20.00
Nappy, 5", bell shape	13.50	Stem, 5 oz., wine goblet	17.50
Nappy, 5", round w/handle	15.50	Stem, 8 oz. water goblet	16.50
Nappy, 7", round	22.50	Stem, parfait	22.50
Nappy, 8½", round	27.50	Sugar w/cover, lacy edge on sugar to serve as	
Nappy, 9", round, 2" high	35.00	spoon holder	35.00
Nappy, 10", bell	40.00	Sugar, 6½"	14.00
Pedestal, base to punch bowl	175.00	Sugar, individual, open	10.00
Pickle	22.00	Sugar, small w/cover	14.00
Pitcher, 16 oz.	45.00	Tid-bit or snack server, 2 tier (dinner and	
Pitcher, 32 oz.	32.50	breakfast plates)	55.00
Planter, 3" x 8½"	32.50	Tid-bit tray, metal handle on dinner plate	45.00
Planter, 4½"	35.00	Toothpick	22.00
Planter, 5" x 9"	37.50	Tray, 9", oval	55.00
Planter, large, wall, 6"	90.00	Tray, 13½", oval	75.00
Planter, small, wall	45.00	Tumbler, 5 oz. juice	22.50
Planter, square	18.00	Tumbler, 6 oz. old fashioned cocktail	16.00
Plate, 6", bread	12.00	Tumbler, 8 oz.	20.00
Plate, 7" salad, w/depressed center	17.50	Tumbler, 12 oz. ice tea	22.50
Plate, 8½", breakfast	20.00	Vase, 6", bell shape	15.00
Plate, 10½", dinner	40.00	Vase, 6½" or celery	40.00
Plate, 14½"	115.00	Vase, 8½", bell shape	25.00
Plate, 18"	150.00	Vase, 9", bell shape	27.50
Puff box or jelly, w/cover	30.00	Vase, 9", crimped top	32.50
Punch set, 15 pc. (13" bowl, 12 punch cups,		Vase, 9½", straight	35.00
pedestal and ladle)	525.00	Vase, 10" bud (size may vary)	10.00
Punch set, 15 pc. (same as above w/11"		Vase, 11", rose (similar to bud vase	
bowl w/o scalloped bottom)	425.00	but bulbous at bottom)	22.50
Relish, 9", 3 part	35.00	Vase, 11½", bell shape	45.00
Salt and pepper, large, flat, pr.	35.00	Vase, 11½", straight	35.00
Salt and pepper, small, ftd., pr.	20.00	Vase, 12", hand blown	175.00
Sauce boat and tray	57.50	Vase, 14", swung (size varies)	15.00
Saucer	8.00	Vase, 15"	27.50
Sherbet, 3¾", low foot	15.00	Vase, 16", swung (size varies)	15.00
Sherbet, 4¾", high foot	16.50	Vase, 18", swung (size varies)	17.50

Please refer to Foreword for pricing information

"Panel Grape"

GIFT SUGGESTIONS TO PLEASE THE DISCRIMINATING

1881
Bowl, Crimp.

1881 Bowl,
Lip. Ftd.

1881 Bowl,
Shallow

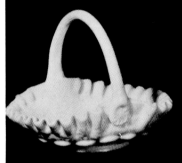

1881
Basket, Hld.

1881
Bowl, Lip.

1881
Bowl, Oval

1881/6½"
Basket

1881
Appetizer Set

1881
Bowl, Bell

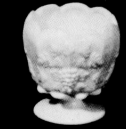

1881
Bowl, Rose

1881
Butter

1881
Bon Bon

3

FAMOUS *"Panel Grape"* THE COLLECTORS FAVORITE

1881 Plates, 14½", 10½" & 8½"

1881
3 pc. Canister Set

1881
Jug, Qt.

1881
Salver, Skirted

1881
Salver, Ftd.

1881 Snack Server

1881
Egg Tray

1881
Ice Tea

1881
Goblet

1881
Sauce Boat/Tray

1881
Mayonnaise

1881
Condiment Set

1881
Salt/Pepper,
Lg.

1881
Oil

1881
Salt/Pepper
(Min. 3 Sets)

1881
Candy

1881
Dish, 3 Ftd.

1881
Puff Box/
Jelly

1881
Chocolate Box

1881
Candy, Crimp.

1881
Pickle

1881
Starter Set

1881
Candlestick

1881
Mayo
Set

1881
Cup/Saucer

1881
Dish, Oval

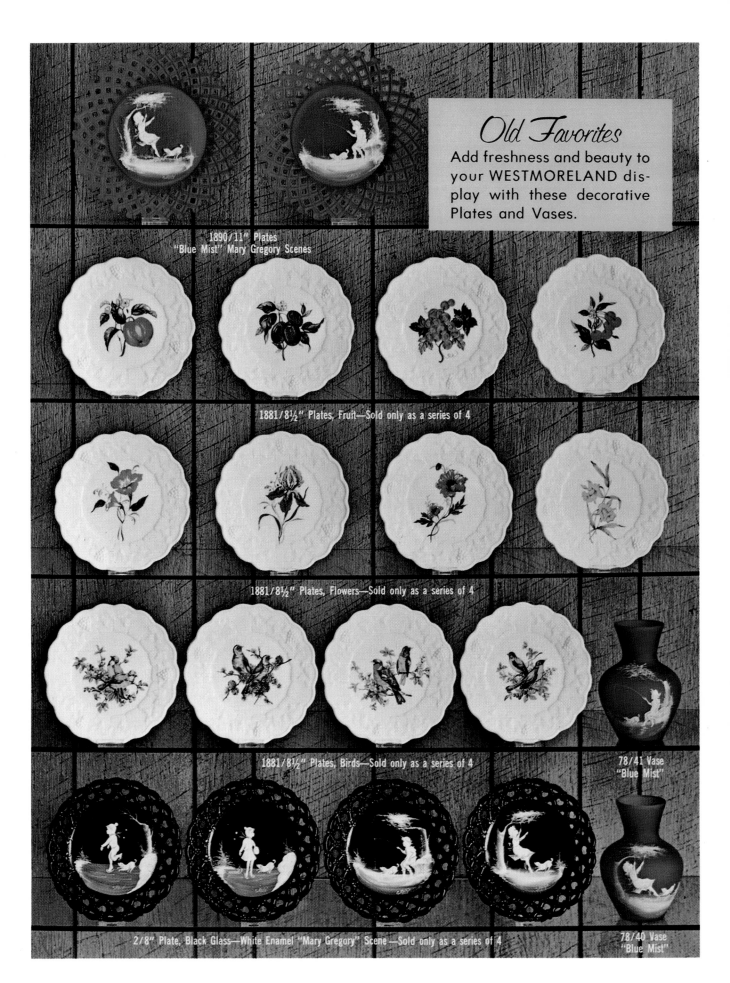

Old Favorites

Add freshness and beauty to your WESTMORELAND display with these decorative Plates and Vases.

1890/11" Plates
"Blue Mist" Mary Gregory Scenes

1881/8½" Plates, Fruit—Sold only as a series of 4

1881/8½" Plates, Flowers—Sold only as a series of 4

78/41 Vase
"Blue Mist"

1881/8½" Plates, Birds—Sold only as a series of 4

2/8" Plate, Black Glass—White Enamel "Mary Gregory" Scene—Sold only as a series of 4

78/40 Vase
"Blue Mist"

"PRETZEL," No. 622 INDIANA GLASS COMPANY, Late 1930's-1980's

Colors: crystal, teal and avocado with recent issues in amber and blue.

Pretzel is another of Indiana's numbered patterns (No. 622) which is better known by its common collectors' name. Be careful buying the celery dishes! Indiana is making them again! They can be found in crystal, amber, blue, and avocado green for $.89 to $1.29 in the local five and dime store; or go to any flea market and you can keep up with all the new issues!

The 4½" fruit cup has been found on a plate that has a 1¼" tab handle. This plate is 6" according to approximately three hundred readers who wrote to tell me. A number of collectors seem to own this plate and I appreciate the information.

Pretzel pieces that have embossed fruit in the center are beginning to sell from twenty to thirty percent more than the plain centered pieces. A few collectors have realized that there is a much smaller supply of these than the plain centered Pretzel.

The pitcher and tumblers are still elusive. There are three sizes of tumblers, but all are equally hard to locate. These, along with the pitcher, are shown in the insert below.

A dated 1955 blue plate with "Virgo" astrology sign on it was found in North Carolina. Has anyone else found anything similar?

Have any of you found any teal Pretzel? I would like to know if you have any in your collections. The cup shown here is still the only piece I am aware of at the present.

	Crystal
Bowl, 4½", fruit cup	4.00
Bowl, 7½", soup	9.00
Bowl, 9⅜", berry	15.00
Celery, 10¼", tray	1.50
Creamer	4.00
*Cup	5.00
Olive, 7", leaf shape	4.00
Pickle, 8½", two hndl.	5.00
Pitcher, 39 oz.	150.00
Plate, 6"	2.00
Plate, 6", tab hndl.	2.50
Plate, 7¼", square, indent	8.50
Plate, 7¼", square, indent 3-part	8.50
Plate, 8⅜", salad	5.00
Plate, 9⅜", dinner	8.00
Plate, 11½", sandwich	10.00
**Saucer	1.00
Sugar	4.00
Tumbler, 5 oz., 3½"	20.00
Tumbler, 9 oz., 4½"	22.00
Tumbler, 12 oz., 5½"	30.00

* Teal - $30.00
**Teal - 10.00

ROYAL RUBY ANCHOR HOCKING GLASS COMPANY, 1938-1960's; 1977

Color: Ruby red.

Royal Ruby is the Anchor Hocking name for their red color. The Royal Ruby sticker appeared on all pieces of red no matter what the pattern may have been. Red Bubble or Sandwich did not mean anything but Royal Ruby to the factory. So, if you find a red piece that seems to be another of Hocking's patterns, do not be surprised by the sticker. Only Anchor Hocking's red can be called Royal Ruby. It is a patented name which can only be used by them!

Although manufacture of Royal Ruby was begun in 1938, most of what is considered Royal Ruby was made after 1940. You will find a Royal Ruby section in my tenth edition of *Collector's Encyclopedia of Depression Glass* covering the pieces made in the 1930's. Speaking of the 1930's, I found a catalogue page that shows that the "card holder" actually was a cigarette box which came with Royal Ruby ash trays. It is probably the most difficult piece to find in this pattern. Royal Ruby will continue to be listed in both books as it cuts into both pre 1940 and post 1940 time periods.

The upright 3 quart pitcher and the 5 ounce, 9 ounce and 13 ounce flat tumblers were listed as the Roly-Poly Line in a 1951 catalogue. That same page shows the Royal Ruby Charm which became just Royal Ruby in future catalogues. As I mentioned under Charm on page 36, Forest Green and Royal Ruby square were not considered to be Charm in subsequent catalogues after they were introduced under that name.

I receive many letters on Royal Ruby beer bottles. There were six or seven sizes of these made for a national beer company in 1949, 1950 and 1963. The date of manufacture is on the bottom of each bottle. You will find '49, '50 or '63 on these bottles. Pictured are 32 ounce (1949) and 12 ounce (1963) bottles. Millions of these bottles were made, but they were too costly and were discontinued. The 16 oz. size is the hardest to find as it was never put into mass production. Bottle collectors seem to find these more attractive than Royal Ruby collectors. I do not consider them dinnerware items, although some collectors might disagree!

Both style sherbets are shown in front of the beer bottles. The stemmed is behind the footed one. Oval vegetable bowls are still in short supply. These are one of the toughest to find pieces in this pattern. Other items in short supply (besides the alias card holder/cigarette box) are the 3 quart upright pitcher, punch bowl base, deep popcorn bowl and the salad bowl with 13¾" underliner.

I finally discovered why so many slotted sugar lids do not fit the sugar bowls. (The lids for the sugars are all slotted for a spoon.) Not all these lids were made for Royal Ruby sugars; some were made for a crystal sugar which is slightly smaller in diameter making its lid unusable on anything else.

I have also listed the crystal stems with Royal Ruby tops called "Boopie" by collectors and the stems that go with Royal Ruby Bubble. See a complete explanation under Bubble on page 10.

Hopefully, you will find this revised listing of Royal Ruby easier to use than previous listings in my earlier books.

	Red			Red
Ash tray, 4½", leaf	3.00	Punch bowl		30.00
Beer bottle, 7 oz.	15.00	Punch bowl base		32.50
Beer bottle, 12 oz.	20.00	Punch cup, 5 oz.		2.50
Beer bottle, 16 oz.	30.00	Saucer , round		1.50
Beer bottle, 32 oz.	25.00	Saucer, 5⅝", square		1.75
Bowl, 4¼", round, fruit	5.00	Sherbet, ftd.		7.50
Bowl, 4¾", square, dessert	6.50	Sherbet, stemmed, 6½ oz.		7.00
Bowl, 5¼", popcorn	11.00	*Stem, 3½ oz., cocktail		7.00
Bowl, 7½", round, soup	11.00	*Stem, 4 oz., juice		9.00
Bowl, 7⅜", square	12.50	Stem, 4½ oz., cocktail		8.00
Bowl, 8", oval, vegetable	35.00	Stem, 5½ oz., juice		10.00
Bowl, 8½", round, large berry	16.00	Stem, 6 oz., sherbet		7.50
Bowl, 10", deep, popcorn	35.00	*Stem, 6 oz., sherbert		7.00
Bowl, 11½", salad	30.00	*Stem, 9 oz., goblet		12.00
Cigarette box/card holder, 6⅛" x 4"	50.00	Stem, 9½ oz., goblet		11.00
Creamer, flat	7.00	*Stem, 14 oz., iced tea		17.50
Creamer, ftd.	8.50	Sugar, flat		7.00
Cup, round	4.50	Sugar, ftd.		6.50
Cup, square	5.50	Sugar, lid		9.00
Goblet, ball stem	9.00	Tumbler, 2½ oz., ftd. wine		12.50
Lamp	30.00	Tumbler, 3½ oz., cocktail		9.50
Pitcher, 3 qt., tilted	32.50	Tumbler, 5 oz., juice, ftd. or flat		5.50
Pitcher, 3 qt., upright	42.50	Tumbler, 9 oz., water		6.00
Pitcher, 42 oz., tilted or straight	27.50	Tumbler, 10 oz., 5", water, ftd.		6.00
Plate, 6¼", sherbet, round	3.00	Tumbler, 12 oz., 6" ftd., tea		14.00
Plate, 7", salad	4.00	Tumbler, 13 oz., iced tea		12.00
Plate, 7¾", salad, round	5.00	Upright		20.00
Plate, 8⅜", square	7.50	Vase, 4", ivy, ball-shaped		4.50
Plate, 9⅛", dinner, round	9.00	Vase, 6⅜", two styles		7.50
Plate, 13¾"	20.00	Vase, 9", two styles		15.00

* "Boopie"

Please refer to Foreword for pricing information

SANDWICH CRYSTAL HOCKING GLASS COMPANY, 1939-1964; 1977

Colors: crystal 1940-1950's.

I have split the crystal Anchor Hocking Sandwich from the colored in order to facilitate writing about each. Royal Ruby sandwich will appear with that pattern in the tenth edition of *The Collector's Encyclopedia of Depression Glass.*

Pieces in crystal which are shy about showing themselves include the little crimped sherbet or custard (shown in the front of the bottom photograph on page 121), the cereal bowl and 9" salad bowl which uses the 12" plate as an underliner. The 5" crimped dessert as listed by Anchor Hocking only measures 4⅞" in some cases. Mould variation makes size listings a major problem! Both this and the crimped sherbet are listed as occasional Sandwich pieces in the 1956 catalogue. I had never seen this listing until my last trip to Anchor Hocking in December of 1990. "Crimped" is the word used for description of these occasional pieces. I know that both are hard to find and this appears to be the only time they were shown in a listing.

Shown below as a pattern shot is a heavy 9" plate with a scalloped rim. It is the only one I have seen; if you have some in your collection, let me know.

Dinner plates and footed tumblers can be found, but it sometimes takes a lot of searching.

Hocking's Sandwich collecting continues to prosper while Indiana's Sandwich does not do as well. Hocking has gone to some trouble to preserve the collectability of their older glassware; however, Indiana did not. Therein lies the difference. Crystal collectors continue to increase the price of this popular pattern. In fact, this may be the most collected crystal pattern in this book outside of Iris.

Remember that Hocking re-introduced a crystal cookie jar in the late 1970's that was much larger than the old. For a comparison of these cookie jars I am enclosing measurements. The newer one is currently selling in the $10.00 range.

	NEW	OLD
Height	10¼"	9¼"
Opening Width	5½"	4⅞"
Diameter/Largest Part	22"	19"

Most pieces that are in short supply continue to be found, but demand keeps absorbing the supply. I always have a large supply of cups, saucers and 8" plates. These were premiums for buying $3.00 (about ten gallons) of gas at Marathon stations in 1964. We had quite a few of these free dishes when we married twenty-eight years ago. The promotion took four weeks for cup and saucers and the next four weeks for the plates.

	Crystal
Bowl, 4⁵⁄₁₆", smooth	5.00
Bowl, 4⅞"/5", crimped dessert	12.50
Bowl, 4⅞", smooth	5.00
Bowl, 5¼", scalloped	7.00
Bowl, 6½", cereal	25.00
Bowl, 6½", smooth	7.00
Bowl, 6½", scalloped	7.00
Bowl, 7", salad	6.50
Bowl, 7¼", scalloped	7.50
Bowl, 8", scalloped	7.50
Bowl, 8¼", oval	6.50
Bowl, 9", salad	22.50
Butter dish, low	37.50
Butter dish bottom	20.00
Butter dish top	17.50
Cookie jar and cover	35.00
Creamer	5.00
Cup, tea or coffee	2.00
Custard cup	3.50
Custard cup, crimped, 5 oz.	12.50
Custard cup liner	12.50
Pitcher, 6", juice	50.00
Pitcher, ½ gal., ice lip	60.00
Plate, 7", dessert	9.00
Plate, 8"	3.00
Plate, 9", dinner	15.00
Plate, 9", indent for punch cup	4.00
Plate, 12", sandwich	17.50
Punch bowl, 9¾"	15.00
Punch bowl stand	20.00
Punch cup	2.00
Saucer	1.00

	Crystal
Sherbet, footed	7.00
Sugar	7.50
Sugar cover	10.00
Tumbler, 3⅜", 3 oz., juice	12.00
Tumbler, 3⁹⁄₁₆", 5 oz., juice	6.00
Tumbler, 9 oz., water	7.50
Tumbler, 9 oz., footed	20.00

Please refer to Foreword for pricing information

SANDWICH COLORS HOCKING GLASS COMPANY, 1939-1964

Colors: Desert Gold 1961-1964   Forest Green 1956-1960's   Pink 1939-1940
        Royal Ruby 1938-1939   White/Ivory (opaque) 1957-1960's

Forest Green is still THE color in demand. For some reason, the green draws rave reviews even with new collectors. Perhaps the Forest Green Sandwich appears more desirable than the plain Forest Green which has numerous fans. Dinner plates at $62.50 do not seem to discourage anyone. I have noticed a lack of saucers recently. There seem to be five cups for every four saucers. You might remember I mentioned that if you see a stack of saucers priced cheaply. Prices for green have risen due to scarcity and demand! For new collectors, I need to add that those five cheaply priced pieces of Forest Green were packed in Mother's oats. Everyone ate oats; so there are literally thousands of those five pieces available today.

I have not mentioned why the pitchers in Forest Green are in short supply for quite a while. It was a matter of poor marketing procedures. Everyone received the juice and water **tumblers** through boxes of oats as mentioned previously. Juice sets and water sets were marketed with a pitcher and six tumblers. Since everyone already had more tumblers than they knew what to do with, no one would buy the complete sets. The sets were returned to Anchor Hocking unsold and the glass was melted down to use for other products.

There are no Forest Green sugar lids and no lid to the cookie jar has ever been found. Employees remember those topless cookies being sold as vases. They must have done well convincing people that they were wonderful vases because so many are seen today!

I have priced the Royal Ruby Sandwich here, but it belongs in the time period of *The Collector' Encyclopedia of Depression Glass* and can now be found in the Royal Ruby section of that book.

There is little demand for pink since only bowls can be found in that color. Amber is beginning to acquire more devotees. The footed amber tumbler is nearly impossible to find! The one in the photograph is the only one I have ever seen, but a few collectors have written that they are finding some of these. The flashed-on blue cup and saucer may have been a special order and there may be additional colors. I have not seen other items with this treatment.

For only $2.89 you could buy the Ivory with gold trim punch bowl set with an oil change and lubrication at Marathon gas stations in my area in 1964. These punch sets were first made in 1957. They were made in Ivory and Ivory trimmed in 22K gold. There seems to be little price differentiation today, but that trimmed in gold seems to be less in demand.

	Desert Gold	Royal Ruby	Forest Green	Pink	Ivory/ White
Bowl, 4⁵⁄₁₆", smooth			3.00		
Bowl, 4⅞", smooth	3.00	15.00		3.50	
Bowl, 5¼", scalloped	6.00	18.00			
Bowl, 5¼", smooth				6.00	
Bowl, 6½", cereal	12.00				
Bowl, 6½", smooth	6.00				
Bowl, 6½", scalloped		25.00	35.00		
Bowl, 7", salad			50.00		
Bowl, 8", scalloped		35.00	60.00	15.00	
Bowl, 9", salad	27.50				
Cookie jar and cover	35.00		*17.50		
Creamer				20.00	
Cup, tea or coffee	3.50		17.00		
Pitcher, 6", juice			110.00		
Pitcher, ½ gal., ice lip			250.00		
Plate, 9", dinner	8.00		62.50		
Plate, 12", sandwich	12.50				
Punch bowl, 9¾"					15.00
Punch bowl stand					12.50
Punch cup					2.00
Saucer	3.00		10.50		
Sugar no cover			22.00		
Tumbler, 3⁹⁄₁₆", 5 oz., juice			3.50		
Tumbler, 9 oz., water			4.25		
Tumbler, 9 oz., footed	75.00				

* no cover

Please refer to Foreword for pricing information

SANDWICH INDIANA GLASS COMPANY, 1920's-1980's

Colors:

Crystal late 1920's-Today	Teal Blue 1950's-1980's	Milk White- mid 1950's
Amber late 1920's-1980's	Red 1933/1969- early 1970's	Smokey Blue 1976-1977

Collecting Indiana's Sandwich pattern thrills some people and more power to them! Most dealers and many collectors avoid it like the plague because of the company's total disregard of protecting old Indiana patterns by continually reissuing them. The pink and green will be priced in the tenth *Collector's Encyclopedia of Depression Glass* since they were made in the 1930's; and although green has been made again, it is a different shade than the original.

Know that Tiara Exclusives took over Sandwich from Indiana with an issue of red in 1969, amber in 1970 and crystal in 1978. Amber, Chantilly green and crystal were made into the late 1980's and may still be in production for all I can find out.

Basically, the list below incorporates the original Sandwich line from the 1920's and the original Tiara listings from the late 1960's and early 1970's. Eventually, I will be forced to add all the Tiara listings throughout the 1970's and 1980's, but not with this initial offering and not without protest.

The mould for the old wine broke and a new one was designed. All the wines made in the last few years are fatter than the earlier ones which were shaped like Iris wines. These older wines are 4½" tall and hold 3 oz. I do not have the measurements on the new wines. (Tiara catalogues list the wine sets with six goblets, but without any dimensions.) They are shaped more like the cocktail in Iris, only taller.

Teal blue and the milk glass white are both products from the 1950's except this was messed up by Tiara making a teal butter dish as an "exclusive" hostess gift which destroyed the $200.00 price tag on the old. The new could be bought for approximately $15.00. The really maddening thing is that all this "new" Sandwich is being touted to prospective buyers as glass that's going to be worth a great deal in the future based on its past history—and the company is steadily destroying those very properties they're using to sell the new glass! Supreme irony!

I can vouch for six items in red Sandwich dating from 1933, i.e. cups, saucers, luncheon plates, water goblets, creamers and sugars. However, in 1969, Tiara Home Products produced red pitchers, 9 oz. goblets, cups, saucers, wines, wine decanters, 13" serving trays, creamers, sugars and salad and dinner plates. Today, there is no difference in pricing the red unless you have some red marked 1933 Chicago World's Fair. This older marked glass will bring a little more due to its being a World's Fair collectible.

Amber and crystal prices are shown, but you must realize that most of the crystal and nearly all of the amber have been made since 1970. Prices below reflect the small amounts of this pattern I see at the flea markets, etc. Usually the seller is a former Tiara "Party Plan" hostess who is out disposing of her additional wares.

	Amber Crystal	Teal Blue	Red		Amber Crystal	Teal Blue	Red
Ash trays(club, spade, heart, dmd shapes, ea.)	3.00			Goblet, 9 oz.	12.50		40.00
Basket, 10", high	30.00			Mayonnaise, ftd.	12.50		
Bowl, 4¼", berry	3.00			Pitcher, 68 oz.	20.00		125.00
Bowl, 6"	3.50			Plate, 6", sherbet	2.50	6.00	
Bowl, 6", hexagonal	4.50	12.50		Plate, 7", bread and butter	3.50		
Bowl, 8½"	10.00			Plate, 8", oval, indent for sherbet		5.00	10.00
Bowl, 9", console	15.00			Plate, 8⅜", luncheon	4.50		17.50
Bowl, 11½", console	18.00			Plate, 10½", dinner	7.50		
Butter dish and cover, domed	20.00	*150.00		Plate, 13", sandwich	12.50	22.50	32.50
Butter dish bottom	5.00	40.00		Puff box	15.00		
Butter dish top	15.00	110.00		Salt and pepper, pr.	15.00		
Candlesticks, 3½", pr.	15.00			Sandwich server, center handle	17.50		45.00
Candlesticks 7", pr.	22.50			Saucer	2.00	4.50	5.00
Creamer	8.50		40.00	Sherbet, 3¼"	5.00	10.00	
Celery, 10½"	15.00			Sugar, large	8.50		40.00
Creamer and sugar on diamond shaped tray	15.00	30.00		Sugar lid for large size	12.50		
Cruet, 6½ oz. and stopper		130.00		Tumbler, 3 oz., footed cocktail	7.00		
				Tumbler, 8 oz., footed water	8.50		
Cup	3.00	7.50	25.00	Tumbler, 12 oz., footed tea	9.50		
Decanter and stopper	20.00		75.00	Wine, 3", 4 oz.	5.50		12.50

*Beware recent vintage sell $20.00

Please refer to Foreword for pricing information

SHELL PINK MILK GLASS JEANNETTE GLASS CO., 1957-1959

Color: opaque pink.

This popular Jeannette pattern was only made for a short two to three year period in the late 1950's. It was called Shell Pink and included pieces from several popular Jeannette lines to enhance marketability. It was designed as "a delicate coloring that blends perfectly with all kinds of flowers."

The photograph shown at the top of page 127 shows the variety of pieces made. The heavy bottomed 9" vase shown in the center is one of the most difficult pieces to find. To aid in identification in the top photo, I would point out that the long handled bowl (on the right behind the round powder jar and in front of the square candy dish) is called a Gondola fruit bowl by Jeannette. The footed bowl on the left is called a Lombardi bowl and was used with a pair of the double candle holders shown in front of it. The two covered bowls on the left are called wedding bowls. The bowl in the right foreground is the Florentine bowl and the one on the left is the Vineyard 12" relish. Maybe I should call this photo an Italian adventure in Shell Pink!

The elusive lazy susan is shown in the top photo of page 128; the base is the part that is almost non-existent. The bottom photograph shows the pieces made for "Napco Ceramics, Cleveland, Ohio." Each piece is marked thus with the numbers quoted in the price list except for the piece with saw tooth edge in the back which only has "Napco, Cleveland." The piece in the front is the candy bottom of a pattern Jeannette called National and made only in crystal in the late 1940's. This candy bottom was promoted as a vase.

At the top of page 129 pieces of other patterns in the book are shown and also all the pieces that depict animals, insects and birds. The "Eagle" candle holder looks more like the same bird on the "Pheasant" bowl; but not so according to Jeannette. That cigarette box with the butterfly finial is rather hard to find in mint condition. There are many of these that have butterfly damaged tops. The price below is for **mint** condition butterfly boxes. The bottom of page 129 shows Thumbprint designed pieces and a pattern that I have called "Feather." The snack tray, snack or punch cup, 15¾" tray, Venetian tray, and punch bowl all fit this pattern. Speaking of the punch bowl reminds me that the original ladle was **pink** plastic and not crystal.

	Opaque Pink		Opaque Pink
Ash tray, butterfly shape	12.50	"Napco" #2255, ftd. bowl w/saw tooth top	20.00
Base, for lazy susan, w/ball bearings	30.00	"Napco" #2256, square comport	12.50
Bowl, 6½", wedding, w/cover	17.50	"National" candy bottom	10.00
Bowl, 8", Pheasant, ftd.	30.00	Pitcher, 24 oz., ftd., Thumbprint	25.00
Bowl, 8", wedding, w/cover	22.50	Powder jar, 4¾", w/cover	27.50
Bowl, 9", ftd., fruit stand, Floragold	20.00	Punch base, 3½", tall	20.00
Bowl, 10", Florentine, ftd.	22.50	Punch bowl, 7½ qt.	40.00
Bowl, 10½", ftd., Holiday	35.00	Punch cup, 5 oz. (also fits snack tray)	5.00
Bowl, 10⅞", 4 ftd., Lombardi, designed center	37.50	Punch ladle, pink plastic	15.00
Bowl, 10⅞", 4 ftd., Lombardi, plain center	22.50	Punch set, 15 pc. (bowl, base, 12 cups, ladle)	135.00
Bowl, 17½", Gondola fruit	20.00	Relish, 12", 4 part, octagonal, Vineyard design	35.00
Cake stand, 10", Harp	25.00	Stem, 5 oz., sherbet, Thumbprint	10.00
Candle holder, 2 light, pr.	30.00	Stem, 8 oz., water goblet, Thumbprint	12.50
Candle holder, Eagle, 3 ftd., pr.	45.00	Sugar cover	10.00
Candy dish w/cover, 6½" high, square	27.50	Sugar, ftd., Baltimore Pear design	8.00
Candy dish, 4 ftd., 5¼", Floragold	20.00	Tray, 7¾" x 10", snack w/cup indent	7.00
Candy jar, 5½", 4 ftd., w/cover, grapes	15.00	Tray, 12½" x 9¾", 2 hndl., Harp	45.00
Celery and relish, 12½", 3 part	40.00	Tray, 13½", lazy susan, 5 part	30.00
Cigarette box, butterfly finial	75.00	Tray, 15¾", 5 part, 2 hndl.	35.00
Compote, 6", Windsor	17.50	Tray, 16½", 6 part, Venetian	27.50
Cookie jar w/cover, 6½" high	75.00	Tray, lazy susan complete w/base	60.00
Creamer, Baltimore Pear design	12.50	Tumbler, 5 oz., juice, ftd., Thumbprint	7.50
Honey jar, beehive shape, notched cover	30.00	Vase, 5", cornucopia	15.00
"Napco" #2249, cross hatch design pot	15.00	Vase, 7"	32.50
"Napco" #2250, ftd. bowl w/berries	15.00	Vase, 9", heavy bottom	50.00

Please refer to Foreword for pricing information

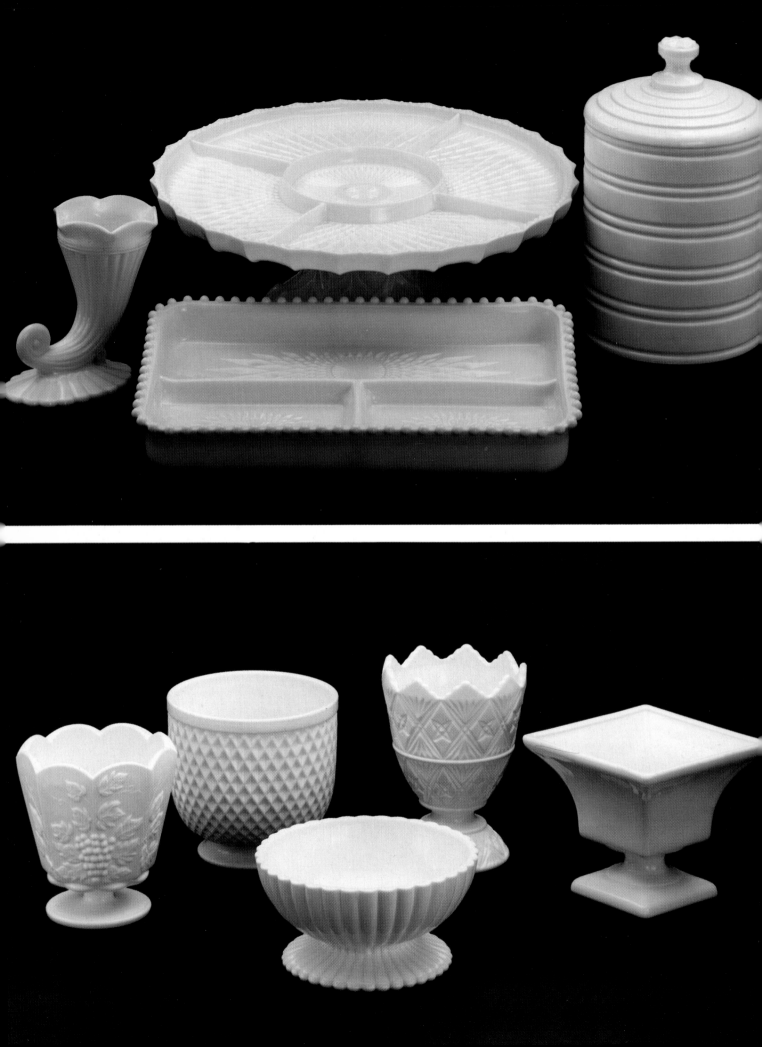

SILVER CREST FENTON ART GLASS COMPANY, 1943-PRESENT

Color: white with crystal edge.

Silver Crest has been one of Fenton's longest running patterns. Every time they drop it out of production, demand forces them to reissue the pattern. Several things will help date your pieces. Before 1958, the white was called opal and has an opalescence to it if you hold it up to the light. In 1958, a formula change to milk glass makes the glass look very white without "fire" in the white. Any pieces reintroduced after 1973 will be signed Fenton. Fenton began signing Carnival pieces in 1971 and in 1973 they continued this practice with all their pieces. If you run into pieces that have white edging, this was called Crystal Crest and dates from 1942.

Some pieces of Silver Crest have two different line numbers on them. Originally, this line was #36 and all pieces carried that designation. In July, 1952, Fenton began issuing a "Ware Number" for each piece. That is why you see two different numbers for some of the different items.

See page 34 for prices on Emerald Crest. Aqua Crest has a blue edge and prices run between that of Silver Crest and Emerald Crest.

	White		White
Basket, 5" hndl., (top hat) #1924	35.00	Candy box #7280	65.00
Basket, 5", hndl. #680	35.00	Candy box, ftd., tall stem #7274	100.00
Basket, 6½", hndl. #7336	35.00	Chip and dip (low bowl w/mayo in center) #7303	60.00
Basket, 7" #7237	25.00	Comport, ftd. #7228	10.00
Basket, 12" #7234	40.00	Comport, ftd., low #7329	17.50
Basket, 13" #7233	60.00	Creamer, reeded hndl. #680	15.00
Basket, hndl. #7339	55.00	Creamer, reeded hndl. (same as #680) #7201	15.00
Bon bon, 5½" #7225	10.00	Creamer, ruffled top	40.00
Bon bon, 8" #7428	10.00	Creamer, straight side #1924	30.00
Bonbon, 5½" #36	10.00	Creamer, threaded hndl. #680	15.00
Bowl, 5½", soup #680	30.00	Cup, reeded hndl. #680, 7209	20.00
Bowl, 5", finger or deep dessert #680	25.00	Cup, threaded look hndl. #680	20.00
Bowl, 7" #7227	17.50	Epergne set, 2 pc. (vase in ftd. bowl) #7202	50.00
Bowl, 8½" #7338	30.00	Epergne set, 3 pc. #7200	100.00
Bowl, 8½" flared #680	30.00	Epergne set, 6 pc. #1522/951	100.00
Bowl, 9½" #682	45.00	Epergne, 2 pc. set #7301	75.00
Bowl, 10" #7224	45.00	Epergne, 4 pc. bowl w/3 horn epergnes #7308	100.00
Bowl, 10" salad #680	45.00	Epergne, 5 pc. bowl w/4 horn epergnes #7305	100.00
Bowl, 11" #5823	45.00	Lamp, hurricane #7398	10.00
Bowl, 13" #7223	45.00	Mayonnaise bowl, #7203	10.00
Bowl, 14" #7323	45.00	Mayonnaise ladle, #7203	5.00
Bowl, banana, high ft. w/upturned sides #7324	60.00	Mayonnaise liner, #7203	25.00
Bowl, banana, low ftd. #5824	45.00	Mayonnaise set, 3 pc. #7203	25.00
Bowl, deep dessert #7221	30.00	Nut, ftd. #7229	10.00
Bowl, dessert, shallow #680	30.00	Nut, ftd. (flattened sherbet) #680	10.00
Bowl, finger or dessert #202	17.50	Oil bottle #680	75.00
Bowl, ftd., (like large, tall comport) #7427	65.00	Pitcher, 70 oz. jug #7467	150.00
Bowl, ftd., tall, square #7330	65.00	Plate, 5½" #680	5.00
Bowl, low dessert #7222	25.00	Plate, 5½", finger bowl liner #7218	5.00
Bowl, shallow #7316	45.00	Plate, 6" #680	6.00
Cake plate, 13" high, ftd. #7213	45.00	Plate, 6½" #680, #7219	10.00
Cake plate, low ftd. #5813	35.00	Plate, 8½" #680, #7217	25.00
Candle holder, 6" tall w/crest on bottom,		Plate, 10" #680	35.00
pr. #7474	50.00	Plate, 10½" #7210	35.00
Candle holder, bulbous base, pr. #1523	25.00	Plate, 11½" #7212	35.00
Candle holder, cornucopia, pr. #951	50.00	Plate, 12" #680	45.00
Candle holder, cornucopia (same as #951),		Plate, 12" #682	45.00
pr. #7274	50.00	Plate, 12½" #7211	45.00
Candle holder, flat saucer base, pr. #680	17.50	Plate, 16", torte 7216	50.00
Candle holder, low, ruffled, pr. #7271	17.50	Punch bowl #7306	200.00
Candle holder, ruffled comport style, pr. #7272	50.00	Punch bowl base #7306	50.00

Please refer to Foreword for pricing information

SILVER CREST (Cont.)

	White		White
Punch cup #7306	10.00	Tray, sandwich #7291	25.00
Punch ladle (clear) #7306	20.00	Tumbler, ftd. #7342	45.00
Punch set, 15 pc. #7306	400.00	Vase, 4½" #203	10.00
Relish, divided #7334	30.00	Vase, 4½" #7254	10.00
Relish, heart, hndl. #7333	20.00	Vase, 4½", double crimped #36, #7354	10.00
Saucer #680, 7209	5.00	Vase, 4½", fan #36	10.00
Shaker, pr. #7206	65.00	Vase, 5" (top hat) #1924	45.00
Sherbert #680	10.00	Vase, 6" #7451	15.00
Sherbet #7226	10.00	Vase, 6", doubled crimped #7156	18.00
Sugar, reeded hndl. #680	15.00	Vase, 6¼", double crimped #36, #7356	15.00
Sugar, reeded hndl. (same as #680) #7201	15.00	Vase, 6¼", fan #36	15.00
Sugar, ruffled top	40.00	Vase, 7" #7455	15.00
Sugar, sans hndls. #680	30.00	Vase, 8" #7453	15.00
Tid-bit, 2 tier (luncheon/dessert plates) #7296	45.00	Vase, 8", bulbous base #186	45.00
Tid-bit, 2 tier (luncheon/dinner plates) #7294	45.00	Vase, 8", doubled crimped #7258	15.00
Tid-bit, 2 tier plates #680	45.00	Vase, 8", wheat #5859	40.00
Tid-bit, 2 tier, ruffled bowl #7394	60.00	Vase, 8½" #7458	45.00
Tid-bit, 3 tier (luncheon/dinner/dessert plates) #7295	45.00	Vase, 9" #7454	45.00
Tid-bit, 3 tier plates #680	45.00	Vase, 9" #7459	45.00
Tid-bit, 3 tier, ruffled bowl #7397	75.00	Vase, 10" #7450	100.00
Top hat, 5" #1924	45.00	Vase, 12" (fan topped) #7262	95.00

SQUARE CAMBRIDGE GLASS COMPANY, 1952-mid 1950's

Colors: crystal, some red, and black.

Cambridge Square is shown in the 1949 Cambridge catalogue as patent pending. This is one of the few patterns made by Cambridge that fits the time period of this book, but I will add others such as Cascade as time and space permit. Be sure to see the advertisement for the Cambridge Glass Club in the back of the book. A few pieces were made in color, but some of these were made by Imperial after Cambridge closed. I will price these later as I obtain some more information on these pieces. The "crackle" tumbler shown in the back left of the bottom photograph sells for $45.00.

	CRYSTAL		CRYSTAL
Ash tray, 3½" #3797/151	6.50	Plate, 9½", tidbit #3797/24	17.50
Ash tray, 6½" #3797/150	8.50	Plate, 11½" #3797/26	22.50
Bon bon, 7" #3797/164	12.50	Plate, 13½" #3797/28	27.50
Bon bon, 8" #3797/47	22.50	Relish, 6½", 2 part #3797/120	15.00
Bowl, 4½", dessert #3797/16	10.00	Relish, 8", 3 part #3797/125	20.00
Bowl, 6½", individual salad #3797/27	12.50	Relish, 10", 3 part #3797/126	22.50
Bowl, 9", salad #3797/49	30.00	Salt and pepper, pr. #3797/76	20.00
Bowl, 10", oval #3797/48	22.50	Saucer, coffee #3797/17	6.50
Bowl, 10", shallow #3797/81	25.00	Saucer, tea #3797/15	6.50
Bowl, 11", salad #3797/57	35.00	Stem, #3798, 5 oz., juice	9.00
Bowl, 12", oval #3797/65	27.50	Stem, #3798, 12 oz., iced tea	11.00
Bowl, 12", shallow #3797/82	32.50	Stem, #3798, cocktail	15.00
Buffet set, 4 pc. (plate, div. bowl, 2 ladles)		Stem, #3798, cordial	22.50
#3797/29	45.00	Stem, #3798, sherbet	10.00
Candle holder, 1¾", block #3797/492, pr.	20.00	Stem, #3798, water goblet	12.00
Candle holder, 2¾", block #3797/493, pr.	22.50	Stem, #3798, wine	17.50
Candle holder, 3¾", block #3797/495, pr.	25.00	Sugar #3797/41	9.00
Candle holder, cupped #3797/67, pr.	22.50	Sugar, individual #3797/40	9.00
Candy box and cover #3797/165	27.50	Tray, 8", oval, for individual sug/cr #3797/37	15.00
Celery, 11" #3797/103	22.50	Tumbler, #3797, 5 oz., juice	12.00
Comport, 6" #3797/54	20.00	Tumbler, #3797, 14 oz., iced tea	15.00
Creamer #3797/41	9.00	Tumbler, #3797, low cocktail	11.50
Creamer, individual #3797/40	9.00	Tumbler, #3797, low cordial	25.00
Cup, coffee, open handle #3797/17	10.00	Tumbler, #3797, low sherbet	9.00
Cup, tea, open handle #3797/15	10.00	Tumbler, #3797, low wine	12.50
Decanter, 32 oz. #3797/85	77.50	Tumbler, #3797, water goblet	12.00
Ice tub, 7½" #3797/34	30.00	Vase, 5½", belled #3797/91	22.50
Icer, cocktail w/liner #3797/18	30.00	Vase, 5", belled #3797/92	20.00
Lamp, hurricane, 2 pc. #3797/68	37.50	Vase, 6" #3797/90	20.00
Mayonnaise set, 3 pc. (bowl, plate, ladle)		Vase, 7½", ftd. #3797/77	20.00
#3797/129	27.50	Vase, 7½", rose bowl #3797/35	30.00
Oil bottle, 4½ oz. #3797/100	18.00	Vase, 8", ftd. #3797/80	17.50
Plate, 6", bread and butter #3797/20	7.50	Vase, 9½", ftd. #3797/78	25.00
Plate, 7", dessert or salad #3797/23	12.00	Vase, 9½", rose bowl #3797/36	40.00
Plate, 7", salad #3797/27	11.00	Vase, 11", ftd. #3797/79	35.00
Plate, 9½", dinner or luncheon #3797/25	25.00		

STARS and STRIPES ANCHOR HOCKING GLASS GLASS COMPANY, 1942

Color: crystal.

This pattern was a derivative of Queen Mary, and I had often wondered if it were a part of that pattern. In any case, in time to salute the American soldiers of Desert Storm, welcome home to the **STARS and STRIPES!** I found a sherbet last week in Florida, but it was too late to include it in the photo.

	Crystal
Plate, 8"	10.00
Sherbet	12.50
Tumbler, 5", 10 oz.	17.50

SWANKY SWIGS 1930's-1950's

Swanky Swigs originally came with a Kraft cheese product in them. Shown here are ones produced from the late 1930's into the 1950's with a bicentennial also shown. Smaller size glasses and the larger 10 oz. size seem to have only been issued in Canada. There is limited availability of these in the states. Tulip No. 2 only turns up on the West Coast and prices are a little less there. Earlier Swanky Swigs can be found in *The Collector's Encyclopedia of Depression Glass* if you get hooked on collecting these. Lids are shown on page 141 as is the plate offered on one lid "for a quarter and two jar labels from Kraft Cheese Spreads." Lids fetch $3.00 up depending upon condition and advertisement!

Page 139:

Row 1: Tulip No.1	blue	4½"	12.50- 15.00
	blue	3½"	3.00- 4.00
	red	4½"	12.50- 15.00
	red	3½"	3.00- 4.00
	green	4½"	12.50- 15.00
	green, black	3½"	3.00- 4.00
	green w/label	3½"	8.00- 10.00
Tulip No.2	red, green	3½"	20.00- 25.00
Row 2: Tulip No. 2	black	3½"	20.00- 25.00
Carnival	yellow, red	3½"	4.00- 6.00
	green, blue	3½"	4.00- 6.00
Tulip No. 3	lt. blue, yellow	3¾"	2.50- 3.50
	dk. blue	4½"	12.50- 15.00
	dk blue	3¾"	2.50- 3.50
	dk. blue	3¼"	7.50- 10.00
Row 3: Tulip No.3	red	4½"	12.50- 15.00
	red	3¾"	2.50- 3.50
Posy: Tulip	red	4½"	12.00- 15.00
	red	3½"	3.00- 4.00
Posy: Jonquil	yellow	4½"	12.00- 15.00
	yellow	3½"	4.00- 5.00
Posy: Violet	purple	4½"	12.50- 15.00
	purple	3½"	4.00- 5.00
	purple	3¼"	7.50- 10.00
Row 4: Cornflower No. 1	lt. blue	4½"	12.50- 15.00
	lt. blue	3½"	4.00- 5.00
	lt. blue	3¼"	7.50- 10.00
Cornflower No. 2	dk. blue	3½"	2.50- 3.50
	lt. blue	3½"	2.50- 3.50
	lt. blue	3¼"	7.50- 10.00
	red, yellow	3½"	2.50- 3.50
	yellow	3¼"	7.50- 10.00

Page 140

Row 1: Forget-Me-Not	dk. blue, blue, red, yellow	3½"	2.50- 3.50
	yellow w/label	3½"	8.00- 10.00
	yellow	3¼"	7.50- 10.00
Daisy	red, white & green	4½"	12.50- 15.00
	red, white & green	3¾"	2.00- 3.00
Daisy	red & white	3¾"	20.00- 25.00
Row 2: Bustling Betsy	all colors	3¾"	3.00- 4.00
	all colors	3¼"	7.50- 10.00
Row 3: Antique Pattern: all designs		3¾"	3.00- 4.00
clock & coal scuttle brown; lamp & kettle blue; coffee grinder & plate green; spinning wheel & bellows red; coffee pot & trivet black; churn & cradle orange		3¼"	7.50- 10.00
Kiddie Cup: cat and rabbit green		4½"	12.50- 15.00
		3¾"	3.00- 4.00
Row 4: Kiddie Cup: all designs		3¼"	7.50- 10.00
bird & elephant red; bear & pig blue; squirrel & deer brown; duck & horse black; dog & rooster orange		3¾"	3.00- 4.00
bird & elephant w/label		3¾"	8.00- 10.00
dog & rooster w/cheese		3¾"	25.00- 30.00
Bicentennial issued in 1975; yellow, red, green		3¾"	3.00- 5.00

Please refer to Foreword for pricing information

A Publication I recommend:

DEPRESSION GLASS DAZE

THE ORIGINAL NATIONAL DEPRESSION GLASS NEWSPAPER

Depression Glass Daze, the original, national monthly newpaper dedicated to the buying, selling and collecting of colored glassware of the 20's and 30's. We average 60 pages each month, filled with feature articles by top-notch columnists, readers' "finds," club happenings, show news, a china corner, a current listing of new glass issues to beware of and a multitude of ads! You can find it in the **DAZE**! Keep up with what's happening in the dee gee world with a subscription to the **DAZE**. Buy, sell or trade from the convenience of your easy chair.

Name_____   Street_____

City_____ State_____ Zip_____

☐ 1 Year - $19.00   ☐ Check Enclosed   ☐ Please bill me

☐ Mastercard   ☐ Visa   (Foreign subscribers - Please add $1.00 per year)

Card No._____ Exp. Date_____

Signature _____

Order to D.G.D., Box 57GF, Otisville, MI 48463-0008 - Please allow 30 days

Books By Gene Florence

Schroeder's Antiques Price Guide

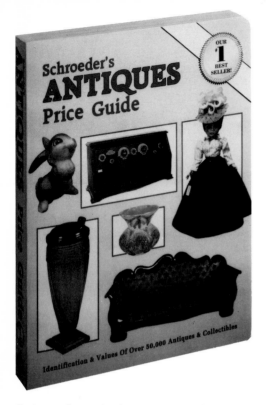

Schroeder's Antiques Price Guide has become THE household name in the antiques & collectibles field. Our team of editors works year around with more than 200 contributors to bring you our #1 best-selling book on antiques & collectibles.

With more than 50,000 items identified & priced, *Schroeder's* is a must for the collector & dealer alike. If it merits the interest of today's collector, you'll find it in *Schroeder's*. Each subject is represented with histories and background information. In addition, hundreds of sharp original photos are used each year to illustrate not only the rare and unusual, but the everyday "fun-type" collectibles as well—not postage stamp pictures, but large close-up shots that show important details clearly.

Our editors compile a new book each year. Never do we merely change prices. Each category is thoroughly checked to spot inconsistencies, listings that may not be entirely reflective of actual market dealings, and lines too vague to be of merit. Only the best of the lot remains for publication. You'll find *Schroeder's Antiques Price Guide* the one to buy for factual information and quality.

8½x11", 608 pages **$12.95**

Collector's Encyclopedia of Depression Glass 10th edition
by Gene Florence

America's No. 1 bestselling glass book has now been produced in an all new special 10th Anniversary edition. It has been nearly 20 years and 10 editions ago since that 1st edition was released in the early 1970's. The special 10th Anniversary edition is bigger and better than ever! Depression glass collecting is at an all-time high as shown by the sales of the 9th edition; we sold 10,000 more copies of the 9th edition than any other previous edition. The all-new 10th edition will be no exception with many new finds being added plus many new photos to bring out the best possible detail for each pattern. Over 5,000 pieces are photographed in full color with complete descriptions and current values included for each piece. A special section is included exposing re-issues and fakes, alerting the buyer as to what has been released and how to determine old valuable glass from worthless new issues. Gene Florence is one of the country's most respected authorities on depression glass. *Kitchen Glassware of the Depression Years, Elegant Glassware of the Depression Era, Pocket Guide to Depression Glass, and Very Rare Glassware of the Depression Years* are among the bestsellers in the country.

No dealer, glass collector or investor can afford not to own this book. It is available from your favorite bookseller for only $19.95. If you are unable to find this book in your area, it is available from Collector Books, P.O. Box 3009, Paducah, Kentucky 42002-3009 for $19.95 plus 2.00 postage & handling.

8½x11", 224 pages HB **$19.95**